I0068090

1,261 Business Development Questions
To Think About As You Grow Your Organization

Version 15.5

By: Kerry James O'Connor

"An Entrepreneur's 'punch-list,' *1,261 Business Development Questions To Think About As You Grow Your Organization*, is a must have for anyone undertaking the challenge of building an enterprise in today's fast moving markets. Covering everything from planning to pricing, this book is a helpful safety check to make sure you really have covered all the bases."

> Jed Emerson
> Bloomberg Senior Fellow
> Harvard Business School

"*1,261 Business Development Questions To Think About As You Grow Your Organization* can help you transform a good idea into a workable reality."

> Gokul Rajaram
> Product Management Director, AdSense,
> Google

"Focus, prioritization, fast and flawless execution – utopia for all managers responsible for leading and growing a business. Kerry O'Connor's primer provides practical solutions for many of the areas that keep managers awake at night."

> Mike Amour
> Chairman & CEO Asia-Pacific
> Grey Group

"Kerry O'Connor has compiled a superb list of business development questions that can help you start or manage a business. It can help focus your thoughts and be a handy reference guide in your business career."

> Tom Watson
> Dean of Omnicom University,
> Former Vice Chairman of
> Omnicom Group

"Effectively managing a billion-dollar health care system requires constant adaptation. *1,261 Business Development Questions To Think About As You Grow Your Organization* serves as an excellent tool for staying focused on what's important."

> Ted Wasson
> CEO/President
> Beaumont Hospitals

Dear Reader:

1,261 Business Development Questions To Think About As You Grow Your Organization is based on 32 year's experience working with clients, conducting research involving hundreds of interviews with senior marketing executives, venture capitalists, entrepreneurs, business school professors and wide variety of other people responsible for successfully developing new products and services across a broad spectrum of businesses.

It is the objective of most entrepreneurs and managers to keep a company alive, and maintain its ability to compete successfully in an appropriately aggressive manner. Survival of the venture is of direct interest to the owners and keeping their jobs is of equal concern to managers who may or may not be part owners of the business. ***1,261 Business Development Questions To Think About As You Grow Your Business*** is written with the early stage of growing a business in mind because the right decisions have to be made if the business is to survive and prosper.

1,261 Business Development Questions To Think About As You Grow Your Business was originally designed for the busy individual who is preparing for an important meeting, to enable the person to ask intelligent questions, and make the meeting a more productive experience for everyone involved.

It isn't intended as a step-by-step guide, because virtually all of the circumstances one encounters in the business world require a dynamic response, meaning your decisions and corresponding actions need to fit the situation in which you find yourself. However, it can do a very good job of helping you stay focused on what is fundamentally important.

The quality of the decisions one makes in business generally fit somewhere on the following line:

(Perfectly)
Awful _____ Perfect

This book was written with the hope that at least a small number of your business decisions will appear further to the right on the line as a result of considering some of the questions in it.

There is nothing sacred about the questions or the sequence in which they appear. Suggestions for improvement are welcome and appreciated. Please contact me at: 1-248-790-8960 or kerryjamesoconnor@gmail.com.

Best wishes for good luck and your success,

Kerry James O'Connor

ISBN #: 978-0-6151-6863-0

© Kerry O'Connor, 1992, 1997, 1998, 2000, 2001, 2003, 2007 All rights reserved. This book, or parts thereof, may not be reproduced in any form without permission from the publisher.

DIRECTORY

Acquisitions 5
Billing & Collections.................................... 5
Capacity of the Plant / Office Site 7
Competitive Assessment............................... 8
Competitors.. 10
Customers – Part A: Business-to-business........... 12
Part B: Consumers (individuals)..................... 16
Database and Knowledge Management............... 17
E-commerce, the Internet and Intranet 18
Evaluating Performance – Customer Satisfaction Research.................. 19
External Barriers to Market Entry.................... 23
Finance..23
Forecasting and Market Development Projections...........................27
Franchising – Part A: Becoming a franchisee............... 28
Part B: Becoming the franchisor....................28
High Volume Production Systems.........................29
Managing The Human Aspects Of Organizational Change To Support
Business Development Efforts............................ 29
Independent Inventory Systems........................ 33
Joint Ventures... 35
Kaizen – Continuous Process Improvement – Development of a
Suggestion System.....................................35
Layout Plant / Office................................... 36
Legal Aspects of Doing Business...................... 36
Location.. 37
Management.. 38
Managerial Staffing..................................... 40
Marketing Research..................................... 43
Marketing and Sales.................................... 44
Materials Management..................................47
Materials / Service Planning 48
New Technologies....................................... 48
Operations as a Competitive Resource................ 49
People.. 51
Pricing...52
Process Design / Process Mapping.................... 53
Production / Work Scheduling..........................54
Product / Service Planning – Assigning Priorities..................54

Production and Staffing...55
Project Scheduling..56
Quality Management...56
Research and Development (R&D)...58
Staff Incentives...58
Strategy and Tactics..60
Suppliers – Sourcing...62
Worker and Operations Scheduling..65
Work Evaluation...66
Business Plan Outline..68

Acquisitions

1) Does it make sense for you to buy a (small) existing business to gain relevant expertise (the related know-how and know-why of how the business works) and an immediate presence in the marketplace? How would the instant creditability, cash flow, marketing/sales connections, borrowing power, store locations, help? What is the down-side to entering the market this way? Before you decide to acquire an existing business, are you taking the time to write down specifically why you are making the acquisition and what you expect to get out of it?

2) How many viable acquisition candidates exist? If new products are crucial to your success, how can ongoing research & development (R&D) activities be continued while your acquisition discussions proceed? How do you intend to address and manage the shift in strategy?

3) If you decide to acquire an ongoing business, who inside your company will be responsible for making the acquisition work? How long will they be assigned to the effort? At what time do you intend to replace the existing management of the company you are acquiring, if you do intend to replace them? If you're pursuing the acquisition to gain expertise, what special effort do you intend to make to retain the people whose expertise you are acquiring?

Billing & Collections

1) Who will have direct daily [primary & secondary/backup] accountability for billing related to the business, product or service?

2) How often can bills be sent out?

3) Can you collect payment when the product is sold or a service is provided? For a service, can you request payment when the service is rendered, or for longer projects, bill at the beginning of the month, or when work commences?

4) Can you request front-side payment at the beginning of a new project? Can you require adequate progress payments to cover your start-up operating expenses?

5) At what point in the month do you plan to get on the phone to track down late payments?

6) What is the industry custom or commonly accepted practice related to billing?

7) Who will be directly responsible and accountable for tracking receivables on a day-to-day basis? Has the responsible person ever held a receivables job involving similar products or services? Does the person have the courage or authority to identify and *red flag* problems, and know there won't be regrettable personal consequences for acting in the best interest of the organization? What kind of specialized knowledge does this person need? What kind of training or mentoring does this person need, if the person lacks the necessary specialized knowledge?

8) Who will ultimately be responsible in management for tracking collections? Can you improve your collection rate and avoid ultimately costly *scorched-earth* situations and unnecessary human tragedies by offering management assistance to customers who lack the expertise to develop 'work-out' plans on their own? When do you plan to make the offer?

9) Who will be responsible for developing a formal credit policy that is clearly understood by your sales, marketing, and business development staff? How will your credit policy compare with other policies in your business segment and that of your competition? Should it be more conservative or more lenient?

10) How much authority will your sales people have to extend credit or discuss your credit policies? Do they understand their limitations?

11) How can you evaluate potential customers on a basis of credit risk? How do you know they pay their bills, or will be able to pay their bills in the future, i.e., in the event of their filing for Chapter 11 protection or declaring bankruptcy? In general, how long do different identifiable customer segments or groups for your products or services normally take to pay their bills?

12) What portion of your inventory or billable hours do you expect to write off annually as non-billable or uncollectible? Who will make the final decision to write off old accounts receivables or inventory, or forego billing for services rendered? What are you basing your decision on, industry standards, past practices? Are anticipated write-offs factored into your financial projections? Is there an opportunity to devise a strategy for dealing more intelligently with the problem than your competitors?

13) How will outside factors affect your ability to collect receivables, i.e., a recession, higher or lower interest rates, government regulations, pending lawsuits, the age or health of your customer, the loss of a major buyer of your customer's services? How can you anticipate the potential impact of these problems and protect your ability to stay in business?

14) At what point will you turn a bill over for outside collection? Is it after the same length of time for all your customers? What level of understanding will your sales staff and operating staff be expected to have regarding your billing and collection policies and the alternatives?

15) Are you willing to factor receivables? At what rate?

16) Will you accept credit card payment, barter arrangements, or a deferred payment schedule? From which sources?

17) How do you intend to control the contracting process and use standardized contract forms and legal language to protect yourself from legal entanglements, including indirect liability for products or services not produced by your organization? If you will be operating in different countries, what additional steps can you take to protect yourself?

18) How will your billing and collection activities in different countries reflect local customs, and how are they likely to impact your cash flow in those regions?

Capacity of the Plant/Office/Store Space

1) How are you defining and measuring your productive capability or capacity?

2) Initially, what is the <u>minimum</u> reasonable size needed for your plant, office, or store?

3) Initially, what is the <u>maximum</u> justifiable size required for your plant, office, or store?

4) How much extra capacity will you need to realistically meet foreseeable demand? How long would it take to increase or find additional, similarly productive plant, office, or store space? How easily can you increase plant, office, or store capacity by re-allocating or borrowing resources from other parts of your organization? Can you work cooperatively with an outside organization to handle your excess work on a subcontracting basis? Can you add extra production shifts? Once you make the decision to expand, how long will it realistically take to bring the new space productively on line?

5) Are you pursuing an aggressive development strategy or a more cautious cash-flow driven strategy? How will your development strategy foreseeably impact your plant, office, or store space requirements?

6) How can you allocate existing working capacity to your short-term opportunities without losing sight of your long-term objectives?

7) Will developing the product or service enable you to eliminate or downsize other locations, or reallocate the unused working capacity to the new product or service?

8) How much plant/office/store maintenance effort will be required as a percentage of your total real estate expenses?

9) Are tax breaks available depending on where you locate your office/facility?

10) How easy would it be for you to close down the location(s) if your situation changes? Do you have a 60 or 90-day escape clause in your various real estate/lease contracts? Can you include them in future contracts?

11) Is there a compelling reason why you need a manufacturing facility or commercial office or store space that is exclusively your own? Do your clients have any interest in visiting your production facilities, office, or store? Have you asked them?

12) Can you locate your production/service/retail facilities on-site at your client's/customer's facilities? Have you discussed the idea with them?

13) Are you prioritizing your capital investments based on the cash flows that will result from the real estate-related expenditures, to avoid tying up your cash on non-revenue producing investments, i.e., administrative buildings, corporate offices, etc.?

14) How many of your people work out of home offices? How do you expect the number of people working out of their homes to change?

15) Who is most productive working out of their home offices? What traits or attributes do these people have that others need to emulate?

16) How do your most profitable competitors manage their real estate commitments?

Competitive Assessment

1) Who are your most successful competitors? What makes them successful, being as specific as possible?   Do they have any traits or attributes that make them competitively unique?

2) Are they as successful today, as they have been in the past?

3) What is your specific competitive objective at the moment -- what things are you seeking to learn from your competitive assessment? Is the information you are seeking already available either on the internet or in some usable form inside your own organization?

4) How will you use the information that you gather? What are you specifically seeking to accomplish with the information you gather? Who else will you share the information with? What other people will use the information from the competitive assessment? What are they seeking to learn, and what will they do with the information? How will they act on it? Who else will be responsible for putting the knowledge derived from the competitive assessment to work? Have you asked the other people who will be using the information for their input, so everyone gets as much value out of the process as possible? Who else in the organization would benefit from having the information that you are seeking to gather? Who else in your organization has information or insight on the subject you're trying to learn more about?

5) Do you intend to use the information for tracking competitive changes in the marketplace? How often do you intend to gather it? How long do you see the need to keep gathering the information? Does it make sense to put a *sunset provision* on the gathering of the information, so you know it won't be mindlessly collected well beyond the time it is actually needed?

6) Who will be responsible for gathering the information for the competitive assessment?

7) How will people inside your organization be made aware the information exists, so you avoid having more than one part of the organization gathering the same information?

8) How will the information that you gather be actively shared inside the organization? Do you intend to put any restrictions on who has access to the information?

9) Can you seek information from the following sources?

- Internet searches using at least three different search engines
- Newspapers, magazines, trade publications/newsletters, foreign publications
- Your competitors' Web sites, and their client's Web sites
- National or International Trade associations, Regional, National, or International Trade shows
- Suppliers
- Mutual customers
- Financial analysts
- Former employees
- Retirees
- Colleagues who are knowledgeable about the competition you're investigating
- Consulting firms
- Past customers
- Market research firms
- Current or prospective customers, manufacturers/service providers
- Distributors, dealers, franchisees, and other channel marketing partners
- Public filings
- Competitors
- Reverse engineering
- Former advertising or public relations agencies or other service providers
- Mystery shoppers, who can evaluate your competition's customer service based on their actual shopping experience

10) What statistical, financial, and operating ratios are available, i.e., 10-K's, 10-Q's, Annual Reports, Value Line Reports, publicly available import/export records, press releases?

11) What projections and forecasts are available for the industry?

12) What industry comparative data is available on your competition?

13) What information is available regarding customer expenditures?

14) What regular market tracking studies are conducted on the industry or service category?

15) What different government sources compile information on this business sector and your competitors?

Competitors

1) Who is your primary competition? Who is your secondary competition?

2) How has the competition changed in your marketplace during the past **2** years? How has the competition changed during the past **5** years? In general, how does the marketplace behave – is the status quo well-defined? Or is the marketplace turbulent, or highly competitive? Have there been any recent changes in the marketplace that leads you to believe now is a particularly good time to enter the marketplace? Have your primary and secondary competitors grown complacent?

3) Do your competitors have significant resources to compete with you in the form of money, access to un-tapped financial resources, unused productive capacity, or coercive influence with government bureaucrats, distributors, dealers, other channel marketing partners and customers? How have your competitors responded to threats in the past? Does your competition have any personal animosity toward you or other competitors? Have there been any recent major changes in your competition's ownership or management that leads you to believe they might respond differently now than they have in the past?

4) If you launch a new product or service not available elsewhere in its current form, how long will you have a competitive advantage in the marketplace before your competitors can develop a competing version of what you're selling? How fast and responsive is your competition? How can you anticipate and plan for your competition's response? Will your competitors cut prices or fees in order to win new business or hold onto existing customers/market share or volume? When you lose or fail to win a major piece of business following open competition, do you make it a point to personally call the decision-maker at the organization whose business you were seeking, to find out specifically why your organization *didn't* get the business, or why your competition *did* get the business?

5) Are you underestimating the anger, intensity and vengeful or mean-spirited nature of your competitors? How has your competition responded in other markets to new entrants? If your major competitor is a large, centralized competitor, and your market is small, do their decision making processes enable them to respond quickly?

6) What is the market's ability to accommodate your new product or service? Is product or service differentiation regarded as a good thing by your prospective customers? Is product or service differentiation [versus standardization] even desirable? Approximately how many products or services can the market support before it becomes overdeveloped and everyone starts losing money?

7) How many competitors offer a similar product or service to your own? How aggressively do they market it? How much value and importance does your *competition* place on product or service differentiation and innovation? [How much do *customers* value the product or service differences?]

8) How stable is the marketplace? Is it dominated by a few large organizations, i.e., multinational, national, regional, or local organizations? Is it spread out more evenly among large and small competitors?

9) How perishable is your product or service from a competitive viewpoint? What is the shelf life or life cycle for your product or service? How does your competition manage their products or services differently, depending on where they are in their life cycles?

10) How big a short/long-term problem is overcapacity due to cyclicality or seasonality? How will a change in pricing strategy by your competition, or some other identifiable factor, impact your ability to compete? How long will it take you to bring new production on-line, or take existing production off-line?

11) How diverse or agile are your competitors in terms of being able to adjust their competitive strategies, brand positioning or brand identities, personality, cultural identities, or image?

12) Do your competitors have different goals and ideas about how to compete so you continually collide with each other in the process? Are there markets they ignore, or pay comparatively little attention to?

13) How significant is your product or service, as a percentage of your prospective customer's total purchases in your product or service category? Do your current and/or prospective customers use different products and/or services interchangeably?

14) How significant are your competition's exit barriers (their cost of getting out of the business) due to specialized/customized assets, other fixed costs, linkages with sister business units, union agreements, joint operating agreements, loyalty to the community, or top management's loyalty to the particular business? Do they regard the similarly competitive products or services they produce to be part of their core business? During the past several years, has a merger or change in your competition's management occurred that will influence how much they value the products or services as part of the total mix they sell?

15) What do other people outside your business segment think of the business you are in?

16) What do they regard as your competition's legitimate strengths and weaknesses?
17) Are you *sure* you know who all your potential competitors are for a specific piece of business? How has the competitive nature of the marketplace changed during the past 6 months? How do you anticipate it will change during the next 12 months?
18) How do you anticipate your competition will change within the next 6 months, 2 years, 5 years, or 10 years?
19) Do your *new* competitors play by the same rules you do? Is there any tangible penalty if they don't?
20) How does your competition effectively use the internet and e-commerce in ways you don't?
21) Do you have competitors who prefer to compete with you remotely by transacting most of their business via telephone and the internet?
22) How easily can your competition match the product or service specifications for what you sell?
23) How much specialized knowledge is required to effectively compete in your business segment?

Customers Part A: business-to-business   Part B: consumers

Part A: business-to-business customers

1) Who are your best customers for your product or service? What are their unique traits or attributes? What are their demographic characteristics, e.g., where do they live, what ethnography are they, what is their annual income, etc.? What are their psychographic traits, e.g., what are their guiding beliefs, motivations and values, and how have they been influenced by their past purchasing behavior? Have you ever asked your customers why they buy from you instead of someone else? Do you *like* your current or prospective customers? Do you share the same beliefs or values? What do your customers' *other suppliers* have to say about them? What do *their customers* have to say about your competition?
2) Will your prospective customers actually purchase your product or service at a price in sufficient volume to enable you to make an adequate profit? Does your customer *need* to buy your product or service to stay in business? Will your potential customers actually *seek* out your product or service? Has your prospective customer ever purchased your product or service? How much missionary or pioneering work will it take for you to close the sale? Do you have the emotional energy, time, money, commitment and patience to make the effort? Does the size of the sale justify the effort?
3) How do your prospective customers organize their buying processes? Do your potential customers always use a Request For Proposal (RFP) process, or seek at

least 3 bids? How does the size of the purchase influence which purchasing methods the customer uses, i.e., are purchases of $10,000 or less, or spot purchases handled differently? Can you bypass some of the more cumbersome purchasing processes and thereby speed up the sales process by reducing the number of products or services you're selling into smaller increments, while increasing the number of invoices that are submitted?

4) How many people in your prospective customer's organization do you have to convince to buy your product or service? Who are the stakeholders, i.e., who is the top person approving the purchase decision, the technical buyer, and the end user(s) by name and title?

5) Who are the stakeholders and scorekeepers inside or outside your organization who can influence your prospective customers to buy your products or services?

- Current customers
- Channel marketing partners
- Suppliers/vendors
- Financial analysts
- Media/trade press
- Market/industry analysts
- Former employees/retirees
- Competitors
- Multinational/ethnic/religious/political affiliations
- Market economists
- Influential bystanders, members of professional associations
- Independent sales representatives
- Members of your Board of Directors/Trustees
- Your banker, venture capital partners, or other financial advisers

What specific information do the appropriate people need to know if they are going to be involved? Should more than one person from your organization be involved with the sales process? *When* should other people be gotten involved with the sales process?

6) How long, realistically, will it take for your prospective customer to make a purchase decision? What is the cycle time – the time it generally takes, following the initial contact, to close the sale? How many sales calls will you need to make?

7) What outside factors could limit your prospective customer's ability to purchase your product or service, i.e., joint operating agreements; are they captive to cyclical contract negotiations if they are involved with a governmental organization or a union? Are there annual/quarterly budgetary issues they follow that you need to be aware of?

8) Are there any government regulatory issues that could restrict your prospective customer's ability to use your product or service, i.e., are there local content rules, or only certain hours of the day that your product can be sold? What about tariffs, or health-related or safety restrictions?

9) How can you clearly demonstrate or prove that you do a better job delivering your product or service than your competition?

10) Can your product or service offer any unique comparative customer benefits which will be seen as valuable by your customers?

11) Are there system development implications and possible set-up problems related to large scale projects that you need to address prior to approaching a large prospective customer? Do you have existing unused capacity? How long will it take you to increase capacity?

12) From a customer perspective, how do the relative costs of providing your new product or service compare to alternative products or services that are currently available and readily accessible from your competition?

13) Regarding whose business you can seek, what are the self-imposed limitations and restrictions on how you sell your new product or service? Will your new product or service cannibalize sales of existing products or services? If your new product or service will cannibalize existing sales, how can you time the introduction to preserve profitability and transition existing customers? Do you have geographic or sales territory restrictions? How are international sales managed?

14) If your new service or product was <u>not</u> in existence, what products or services would your prospective customers use instead? What are your customer's switchover costs? During the first 12 months, how many of the old products or services will no longer be required? Historically, how loyal have your current and/or prospective customers been to suppliers/vendors?

15) Does your prospective customer have a process they follow when evaluating **new** services or products? Does your organization meet *all* the criteria and does your prospective customer know it? If your organization doesn't meet all the criteria, how much of a problem is it? What un-related factors can you draw upon, that may help you close the sale? Does your business have special status as a minority-owned business; can you benefit from 'local' content requirements?

16) Does your prospective customer have a process they follow when evaluating existing services or products that are delivered in new ways?

17) Is a copy of the prospective customer's purchasing standards or protocols used to evaluate new products or services available in the form of existing contracts, or stated policy? Who is involved in the approval process? Who has been involved in the past?

18) What favorable criteria does your prospective customer use to evaluate development plans for diversifying its supplier/vendor base?

19) From your current customer's perspective, what short-term and long-term opportunities exist to improve administrative or operating efficiencies between your two organizations?

20) What are the two or three key factors your potential customer will focus on to make the buying decision? How do these key buying factors relate to the technical performance or design of your products or service staffing related to each alternative? How do they relate to intangible factors, i.e., creative ability, dislike of other suppliers, etc.?

21) Is there agreement on the relationship between buying criteria and product/service design? How are production and staffing variables being taken into consideration? How do those compare with what your competition can provide?

22) How closely can you meet the most important factors related to your prospective customer's specific motivating purchase decision-criteria? Are you missing any? How have you compensated for them?

23) How much opportunity is there to incrementally improve product or service quality or increase production? Will your competition match your effort?

24) How much will the prospective customer value the full scale potential of your product or service? How much will it cost you in time, effort, and money to reach full scale? Does the probable life cycle of the product or service justify the effort?

25) How do customers see your product or service in comparison with competing products or services? How do you know? What quantitative data or outside sources of impartial information do you have? Is there any reason you can't ask your current or prospective customers for honest feedback?

26) What significant problems or sources of dissatisfaction do prospective customers have with your competitor's product or service that are sufficiently annoying to cause them to switch suppliers?

27) Will the customers you have today be the customers you are most likely to have a year from now, 2 or 3 years from now? Is there a commonly accepted industry standard for how long supplier relationships generally last, i.e., five years, etc.?

28) How do your customers define quality? How can you encourage adoption of a single set of quality standards or benchmarks inside your organization?

29) If you will be dealing with sourcing people or others who don't have an integral understanding of your products or services, what do you need to educate them, so they can make a favorable decision in your behalf?

30) Can you develop 3 fairly standardized proposals (templates) for describing your deliverable in specific terms, so your prospective customer has a better understanding of what they are getting in tangible terms?

31) From a customer perspective, how important is it for your product or service to be scalable?

Part B: Consumers (individuals)

32) How trendy, perishable or durable is your product or service? What is the typical life cycle for products of services in the marketplace?

33) How much of an impulse purchase is your product or service it? How silly or impulse-driven, or desperate is your prospective customer?

31) Does your customer *need* your product or service? How many reasonable alternatives to your product or service can your consumer find?

32) How effectively (being as specific as possible) does your competition currently satisfy the needs or interests of your prospective customers?

33) Does your competition take some or all of its customers for granted? Does it virtually ignore some of them?

34) How much do your prospective customers know about what you sell? Are they very limited in what they buy, or will they actually buy many more, different varieties of what you are selling, if you produce greater variety? Will they buy different varieties in sufficient quantity to make the effort worthwhile?

35) What are the unique traits or attributes of the people who buy your products or services?

36) What does your prime prospect look like, i.e., can you put a picture up on your wall of who your prime prospect is, so you can stay focused on making sure you are meeting the wants needs or desires of that particular customer?

37) How are the traits or attributes of your customers changing? Are the decision-makers more ethnically diverse in their backgrounds than in the past? How are their wants, needs and desires changing, and how does what you sell reflect that?

38) At what time of the day, are people most interested in shopping for, and buying your product or service? How does your staffing or availability accommodate your customers' shopping preferences?

39) How many different ways can your current and best prospective customers reach you, i.e., by coming to your store when it is open, by using the internet, cell phone, 24-hour call service?

40) How price sensitive is your customer?

41) How much follow-up service will your customers want or require? How profitable can the after-market service aspects of your business be?

42) Typically, how old is your best prospective customer?

43) Will your customers buy enough of your product or service to enable you to make a profit, and stay in business?

44) How important is the physical location of your store or service?

45) Are there governmental restraints (zoning, regulatory, environmental restrictions) on where your business can operate?

46) Do your customers buy from you for intangible reasons, i.e., tradition?

47) How does seasonality influence when your customers decide to purchase your product or service? Are there other complementary products or services that you can offer?

Database & Knowledge Management

One of the most valuable things a company possesses is its knowledge of its customers, prospective customers, and the dynamics of the marketplace. Essentially, this amounts to a collective database of knowledge. How well this knowledge is managed, protected, and nurtured determines how effectively a company is able to grow its business, by introducing relevant new products and services, and successfully responding to changes in the marketplace. The value of a company's database of knowledge depends on how current, accurate, and accessible it is
to the people who need the information.

1) Who is going to organize and grow your organization's knowledge center?

2) What processes will be used to gather the information for the database, i.e., by regular debriefings, case studies, exit interviews? Who will be assigned to gather the information?

3) How will the information be shared with people? Do you intend to restrict who has access to parts of the information?

4) Do you intend to evaluate how frequently and effectively people inside the company use the knowledge center?

5) How do you intend to make sure the information is kept current?

6) Can you actually consolidate all of the information that belongs in one knowledge center in one place that everyone uses?

7) How do you intend to encourage the continuing professional development of your employees, by sharing the information with them in the database/ knowledge center?

8) How do you encourage people to share their ideas to continuously improve your organization? How are the ideas captured in the database/knowledge center?

9) How do you intend to reward or acknowledge new ideas added to the database/knowledge center?

10) How do you intend to reward or acknowledge people's efforts to continue to improve themselves by using the database/knowledge center?

© Kerry O'Connor 1992, 1997, 1998, 2000, 2001, 2003, 2007

E-commerce, the Internet & Intranets

1) Who among the end users inside your company (marketing, sales, operations, finance) has direct responsibility and accountability for making sure your e-commerce, internet-based, and internal Intranet systems are developing in a relevant, highest priority-driven manner, that supports cash flow and demonstrable economic gains from improvements to operating efficiencies. How is the ROI on the decisions going to be tracked, and who is going to be held responsible and accountable for tracking them?

2) Who will have *ultimate authority* in senior management to establish *e-commerce* development and content priorities? How will this person's authority be supported by other members of top management? How can you protect this person from having to allocate precious resources to the 'pet projects' of senior managers?

3) Who will have *ultimate authority* in senior management to decide **intranet** (inside the company involving communication with other parts of the company) development and content priorities? How will this person's authority be supported by other members of top management to support ongoing operating activities?

4) Do you have the opportunity to go on-site visits to organizations whose work in the, *e-commerce* area, you admire? Who should be part of the group that go on the site visits, i.e., end users, people involved with your information technology & telecommunications systems, operations, finance, strategic development, marketing, advertising & sales, and/or customer service?

5) As an organization, how can you challenge your own assumptions regarding the importance of *e-commerce* in your overall development strategy? If *e-commerce* activities are replacing other communication or transactional mediums, how do current resource allocations reflect the shift? Who is best-suited to play a leadership role to meet future challenges? How can this person's efforts be supported by top management, and specifically who will this person work most closely with in senior management?

6) What other organizations would you be wise to reach out to, to seek advice about how to develop your *intranet* system? Have you sought the suggestions of end users across multiple levels of the organizations involved with operations, information technology & telecommunications systems, shipping and receiving, purchasing, finance & accounting, customer relations management/service, marketing, advertising & sales?

7) How can you encourage the people responsible for both your internet and intranet activities to look for high value opportunities that may exist, and spare them from allocating resources based on anachronistic (out-of-date, of questionable relevance) small-minded decision-making models based on organizational politics?

8) How does your *intranet* development strategy support your intention to preserve as much value and usefulness as you can from past (legacy) systems while transitioning to commonly accepted industry standards when acquiring new management information system technology? If you are bringing a new information system on-line, how can you avoid the potentially catastrophic risk of bringing a new and un-proven *intranet* operating system on-line? Can you bring the new system on-line in parallel with the old system in the event of an unforeseen system failure? Does it make sense to bring parts of your *intranet* system on-line before others, to avoid potential problems that could interrupt cash flow, or severely damage customer relations?

9) Who will be given the use of expensive personal wireless communication devices inside the company? Have you asked people for their communication preferences? If wireless resources are the preferred method of communication, what other expenditures or resources can be eliminated?

Evaluating Performance – Customer Satisfaction Research

The best reason for evaluating your company's performance on a regular basis is:

- To identify problems, before your on-going business relationships become terminal cases, or your ability to gain new customers is impaired. It can also be useful for identifying opportunities for improvement that may translate into a competitive advantage.
- To identify new business opportunities.

In the long run, you will come out far ahead by regularly evaluating your organizational performance in a relevant manner that addresses your specific interests, and those of other stakeholders and scorekeepers involved with your business. You may also be able to prevent a few human tragedies, by moving otherwise productive and/or loyal people who are burned out from working too long on one product or service to another line of business, before insurmountable problems arise. *One example of a customer satisfaction survey developed by Bellwether Leadership Research & Development is included at the end of this section.*

Most organizations evaluate their performance in one of three ways. Depending on the number of customers you have, you can do it yourself 'live and in person' by regularly calling on your customers. Or you can use letters and/or email questionnaires that can be sent to each customer or a core sampling of customers. Finally, a trusted, impartial outside organization can collect the information for you.

Having top managers of your organization talk directly with your most important customers, offers the added benefit that if one of your customers is about to end the working relationship or drastically curtail it, your manager is in the best position to respond immediately. The down-side for your managers is the process can be very time consuming, and your customers may start routinely calling your senior managers when they have minor problems, essentially turning them into highly paid traffic cops.

1) Are you talking with customers, employees, franchisees, joint venture partners, suppliers and investors and encouraging them to disclose problems?

2) What criteria should you use to evaluate the performance of your service or product and your organization that will produce meaningful feedback and identify underlying problems or opportunities? How is the criteria you're using relevant to how your customers evaluate your product or service?

3) How do competing organizations evaluate their own performance?

4) If written evaluations are used, what are you doing to avoid situations where the person/division is having problems that aren't being addressed by the evaluation process, i.e., is the person/division being given glowing reviews, because the person's/division's boss is trying to avoid confrontation even as the problems grow more difficult to fix?

5) How often do you intend to personally evaluate your own performance on a organized basis that can be tracked and quantified? How will you follow up on the information? Who will be responsible?

6) How can you constantly monitor the reality of your situation, and make adjustments when necessary?

(Example)

Dear XXXXXX,   **Date**

In an effort to improve XXXXXXXXXX's work for you, and make sure we are living up to your expectations, I am writing to ask if you would be kind enough to let me know how well XXXXXXXXXX is currently performing its work for you. To facilitate the process, I have attached several questions.

If you would prefer to speak directly, my phone number is XXXXXXXXXX.

Thank you for your help.

Sincerely,

XXXXXXXXXXXX

How is XXXXXXXXXXX performing its work for you from your perspective in the following areas?

Professionalism (overall approach to how we work with you):

1--10
Bad   Excellent

Comments:
                                             *

Attention to detail (timeliness and cost tracking, financial and project control, etc.):

1--10
Bad   Excellent

Comments:
                                             *

Quality and consistency across products/services:

1--10
Bad   Excellent

Comments:
                                             *

Quality of our strategic, analytical, reasoning, and problem-solving skills:

1--10
Bad   Excellent

Comments:
                                             *

Quality of XXXXXXXXX's creative work:

1--10
Bad   Excellent

Comments:
                                             *

Compared to other organizations with whom you work, how would you rate XXXXXXXXXXXX?

1--10
Bad   Excellent

Comments:

*

How would you rate XXXXXXXXXXX's overall performance?

1--10
Bad   Excellent

Comments:

*

How do you feel regarding the following statements?

	False	True	Sometimes
XXXXXXXXXX doesn't challenge us enough	_____	_____	_____
XXXXXXXX just shows us what we expect to see	_____	_____	_____
The creative team demonstrates a good understanding of our business	_____	_____	_____
We have clear, open channels of communication with the account team	_____	_____	_____

How can we improve? Do you have suggestions for how XXXXXXXXXXXXX can improve that aren't covered elsewhere?

Suggestions: _____

Completed by: _____

Can someone call you regarding your responses? Yes _____ **No** _____

Please call this person instead: _____

External Barriers to Market Entry

External barriers to entry are obstacles that make starting a business less attractive as an opportunity, and may serve to protect existing businesses.

1) How difficult would it be for a new competitor to enter into your line of business and go after the most profitable part of your business? How easy would it be for a new competitor to achieve economies of scale that would threaten your ability to stay competitive in the near future? How has the competitive environment changed during the past 6 months? Are external barriers to entry higher or lower than they were 6 months ago?

2) How important is product or service differentiation in your business sector?

3) What are the switching costs for your current or prospective customers? Are they tied to long-term contracts? How difficult or aggravating would it be for them to switch suppliers, or where they normally shop?

4) At a minimum, how much would it cost and how long would it take for a competitor to enter your line of business locally regionally, or nationally?

5) What portion of your competitor's costs could be salvaged in a distress situation, if they decide to exit the business?

6) What are the cost disadvantages independent of scale to entering your line of business?

7) Can new competitors gain adequate access to distribution channels to achieve throughput requirements and financial returns to justify getting into the business?

8) Are government policies or regulatory trade barriers sufficiently high to make your new competitor's ability to enter the market very difficult, or get out of the business, i.e., due to costs of environmental (cleanup) issues, pending lawsuits, or pension funding obligations?

9) What outside factors could raise or lower the outside barriers to entry, i.e., a change in technology, import/export tariffs, outsourcing labor intensive activities, better roads, ports, etc.?

Finance

1) What is the economic justification for your new product or service? Has a feasibility study been conducted that includes a cost-benefit and breakeven analysis?

2) Will the new product or service replace existing products or services that have become obsolete involving plant and equipment that is fully depreciated? If you bring this new line of products or services on-line, are you taking other products or services off-line? How can you time the new product/service introduction to your best financial advantage? If you decide to go ahead with development, are you bringing your productive capacity on-line first, versus building administrative offices (non-productive overhead), that can be built after you go on-line, to take advantage of the cash flow from the new production?

3) Are you developing your new products or services to meet existing needs, or do they represent an opportunity to generate revenue from totally new markets? Can you utilize existing volume in replacement studies? What methods are you using to estimate volumes and expansion of existing products or services? Have you identified the customer mix represented by volumes and analyzed the reimbursement implications associated with the various customers? If this is a pass-through product or service for existing customers, has the purchase been evaluated to determine to what extent your customers are willing to pay for it? Have you spoken with *all* the appropriate current or prospective customers? If existing customers won't pay for this product or service, what impact will this have on revenue projections? Will the product or service result in verifiably lower operating costs for your organization; have other similarly configured businesses been able to demonstrate a verifiable savings in operating expenses?

4) What financial pressure will this new product or service put on existing resources? Will additional staff or equipment be required? At what cost? What are the variable expenses (labor, supplies, etc.)? What additional capital will be required? What incremental indirect expenses, based on scale, will be incurred?

5) Have you evaluated the reasonableness of volume projections, given organizational capacities? Is there sufficient operating capacity to accommodate incremental business? What kind of capacity? Is there capacity to accommodate incremental increases in certain kinds of business? If yes, for what type(s)?

6) How will this new product or service expand ancillary volume?

7) Have you evaluated the impact the new product or service will have on overall operations? Have you evaluated the impact of capital acquisitions on existing products or services, or considered how existing capacity can be made more efficient through scheduling or other means?

8) What are the implications related to:

- Competitive position (locally, regionally, nationally, multinationally)
- Pricing sensitivity
- Customer mix
- How well the new business fits into your core long-range strategy
- Financing, legal implications
- Level of senior management involvement and impact on organizational structure
- Billing and information services requirements

9) Have you assessed the investment in terms of impact on cash flow, net present value (NPV), etc.?

10) How is the introduction of the new product or service consistent with the organization's strategic goals?

11) How does this investment opportunity compare with others you are considering?

12) How have you assessed the financial risk of the project? What is the extent of your financial exposure associated with the introduction of the new product or service?

13) Have you asked an impartial, outside expert to evaluate your financial assumptions and the alternatives to pursuing the current opportunity being considered? How have other organizations responded to similar opportunities?

14) What are the throughput requirements for the new product or service? How many current or prospective customers do you need to have buy your product or put through the service? If you're making 40% on each unit provided, how many units do you have to put through in three to five years to justify the effort? Are there enough workable hours in the day to meet the throughput requirements? Are there enough customers you can economically reach/sell in order to make this product or service a success?

15) Have you attempted to evaluate the reasonableness of your volume projections in view of recent market analyses which have been conducted? Have you asked an impartial outside expert to "reality check" your sales and marketing assumptions?

16) What types of non-traditional tools may be appropriate for evaluating the investment?

17) Are you overlooking other investments of greater strategic importance? How do you assign priority?

18) Do the numbers tell the whole story? Whose numbers are you using? What part of your estimates and assumptions don't lend themselves to being quantified? Is your investment vulnerable to technical attack, rapid obsolescence, loss of key staff members or other factors beyond your control? Do you actually have contingency plans?

19) Related to evaluating the opportunity, is there open and frequent communication between the development, finance, technical, marketing, sales, and operating staffs? To what extent are they in agreement? To what extent are they willing to commit themselves to the venture? Even with the best of intentions, to what extent will they be able to adequately commit themselves and provide sufficient support to the new venture, in light of their other responsibilities, to reach your objectives? Will dedicated staff be assigned on a full-time basis?

20) How long will your opportunity be available? What is its life cycle and how does it measure up compared to your other opportunities?

21) What share of your (historical) market do you need to capture to make this a feasible product or service?

22) Have you completed **12-month** cash flow projections using different pricing variables, economic scenarios, and market demand?

23) Have you completed **5-year** cash flow projections using different pricing variables, economic scenarios, and market demand?

24) What are the financial barriers to market entry associated with introducing the product or service?

25) How much control do you have over pricing? How long will it last?

26) What are the upside/downside business risks? How can these be recognized and managed?

27) What is the opportunity cost associated with developing this product or service?

28) What does the projected income statement look like:

- Sales
- Cost of Goods
- Operating Expenses
- Depreciation
- Interest Income
- Taxes

29) What is the salvage value of the venture if it turns out badly?

30) What does the projected balance sheet look like:

- Accounts Receivable
- Inventory
- Plant/Office space/Retail stores, Property, Equipment
- Accounts Payable
- Accrued Expenses

31) How do you intend to raise capital, i.e., existing cash flow, venture capital, loans from banks against inventory, receivables, equipment, real estate?

32) Are you willing or able to harvest this venture or liquidate it, if the ROI/reimbursement becomes unfavorable? Who will make *that* final decision?

33) Who are the constituencies for whom value must be created or added to achieve a positive cash flow?

34) What options have you considered for structuring the proposed project, ranging from building the whole thing from scratch to purchasing an existing venture, entering into a shared risk/joint venture, etc.? Are there important tax consequences of different arrangements?

35) What is the legal process and what are the key issues involved in raising outside capital? What factors are *controllable?* What outside factors <u>can't</u> you control?

36) What are some of the bigger, more difficult problems that can be anticipated, prepared for, and responded to? How could they affect your financial returns?

37) How do your projections compare to commonly accepted industry hurdle rates and operating ratios related to ROI in this business category?

38) Historically, how price sensitive has the market been? Why is it likely to change?

39) Have you developed an early warning system to identify problems quickly, so corrective measures can be taken?

40) Are your costs of developing this product or service increasing or falling?

41) Will you be getting a 40% return on your money in the fifth year?

Forecasting & Market Development Projections

1) What role does forecasting play in your efforts?

2) What methods are you using?

3) What different methods have you tried?

4) How are the forecasting methods you use different from those your competitors use?

5) Are your competitors using different forecasting methods and reaching different conclusions?

6) What is the respective historical strength of each forecasting method? What are the shortcomings of each method? What are the associated financial risks of depending on one method, versus using several different methods to challenge your different assumptions?

7) What is the potential impact on your organization of choosing the wrong forecasting model(s), and basing your business development assumptions on the results?

8) What is the historical accuracy using a particular method? If a method is new to you, have you spoken with someone else who has used it? How accurate was it? Has an impartial and respected 'outsider' checked your assumptions and forecasting model for accuracy/validity?

9) On a day-to-day basis, are there simple, reliable methods you can use to forecast demand for your products or services?

10) What sort of controls or constraints do you need to impose on the forecasting system?

11) When you look comparatively at other businesses, who has timed their development efforts most successfully in forecasting how specific markets would develop? Were they consistently successful at forecasting the market's development, or just lucky that things turned out the way they did?

12) Do you plan to go back and validate the accuracy of the *forecasting model(s)* you use? How will you share what you learn with the appropriate people?

13) Do you plan to go back and check how accurate your business development assumptions were, and share the information with your colleagues involved with current development planning? How?

14) Who will be held accountable and ultimately responsible for the accuracy of your forecasting models?

Franchising

Part A: Becoming a franchisee:

1) What expertise do you lack that is easily accessible to you as a franchisee?

2) What are your strengths and weaknesses from a managerial perspective? Would being a franchisee spare you from doing some things you just don't like to do, or aren't good at?

3) Will becoming a franchisee enable you to enter the market sooner?

4) What is the down-side to becoming a franchisee? Are you giving up profit you could easily be holding on to?

5) How much do you know about the franchisor? How well do they work with people like you? What working relationships have been most successful from a franchisee/franchisor perspective in the past?

6) How much can you learn about how the franchisor works with its franchisees before you make a commitment? Can you get your own references?

7) What can you learn from doing internet searches about the franchisor's past business practices?

8) What assumptions are you making? Why are you making them?

Part B: Being the Franchisor: Franchising your products and/or services:

9) Do you have a comparatively unique product or service that people want to be identified with and will buy as a franchisee? Do you have a marketable expertise that people with money value?

10) Do you have creative abilities or other forms of intellectual property that other people greatly admire? Will they pay to be part of a business venture of your creation? How sustainable is your creative ability?

11) If you have a business partner or outside advisors, do they have experience being either a franchisor or franchisee?

12) Do you intend to operate any of the franchises?

13) Who is going to develop your sales prospectus for persuading prospective franchisees to invest in your business?

High-Volume Production Systems

1) Under what circumstances can you use 'just-in-time' scheduling effectively? Can more effective scheduling minimize down cycles and/or over-time, reduce the cost of raw materials, or cut down on shipping costs? How quickly can you increase your production volumes while maintaining acceptable product quality?

2) Have you considered the limitations of production capacity on your system, and evaluated alternative 'make or buy' strategies? How do your best-in-class competitors manage fluctuations in their production – how do they deal with their capacity challenges?

3) How can you use planning to incorporate high volume production in future projects?

4) How can you use outside sources to rapidly increase your production capacity?

5) Would your quasi-competitors be willing to act as your suppliers for large contracts, thereby enabling you to seek business from customers who might otherwise regard you as too small? Are you willing to sign non-compete and non-disclosure agreements?

6) Are you ignoring small, more profitable production contracts, in order to focus on high volume production runs? Do smaller, more profitable production runs serve to smooth out variances in the overall productivity of your operating system? Do your production people like having the extra work? Is it interesting or challenging? Does taking on the smaller production runs represent a hedge against potential financial overexposure to a too narrow product line or small number of clients?

7) How can you reduce your setup/switchover times?

8) Which of your production runs are most profitable? Does your production staff know, and assign production priorities accordingly?

Managing The Human Aspects Of Organizational Change To Support Business Development Efforts

One of the most difficult things any person ever deals with is uncertainty. By its very nature, any form of development involves some form of uncertainty, even if, in Darwinian terms, it *only* unleashes the laws of unintended consequences. Put another way, just about any form of change that can be perceived as a risk or a threat by someone.

Risk adverse people may not be the best people to have involved with business development efforts even if their seniority indicates they are in line for the job. A brave talking person with two children headed into college may consciously or unconsciously be afraid of making one wrong decision, getting fired, and at least in the person's mind destroy his or her children's chance to attend college; therefore, the person will avoid making any decisions at all, or only the safest of decisions where no accountability or responsibility is involved. These people, even with the best of intentions, may not be best-suited for the role of development project leaders, particularly during periods of uncertainty.

Related to business development challenges, before you go through a major product or service launch, acquire another organization or go through a major reorganization, carefully consider on a person-by-person basis who has the right temperament, courage or decisiveness – and the necessary leadership or team-building skills to make the anticipated project a success.

1) What organizational changes will your business development efforts require? Why is this the best time to make the changes? When other companies have made similar changes, what were the results? Have you spoken with people inside those companies to ask for suggestions? What would they have done differently? Have you asked them what they think they did well?

2) How can you rehearse people through the changes your developmental efforts are likely to cause?

3) How are you going to explain to *everyone* inside the organization why the development changes being made are necessary at this time?

4) Have you evaluated different operating scenarios and thoughtfully identified what tangible and intangible things people are likely to gain or lose as a result of your development effort, including what you and your own staff are likely to lose? How can you implement the most disruptive changes quickly to reduce uncertainty, so the largest possible number of people can see immediate benefits?

5) How can you minimize the emotional and financial impact of the changes on your key people [and their families]?

6) Who are the most important people in the organization who *actually* get the work done? If they leave the organization directly or indirectly as a result of the development changes, how will it impact your plans? How can you make a special effort to retain the people?

Developmental changes cause uncertainty for many people in an organization. Two of the best strategies for minimizing uncertainty are to:

- Communicate, communicate, communicate, and keep communicating long after you think it should be necessary; don't expect everyone to respond to the changes rationally; even minor changes can cause significant levels of anxiety in otherwise rational people; people who adapt most easily to uncertainty are

those who feel some sense of control, or have been educated or otherwise trained to adapt to change.
- Keep people busy; empower people to keep everyday work processes flowing.

7) With a major acquisition, how clear will the operating guidelines be from the start?

8) Regarding sources of confusion, which circumstances will be *controllable* and which events will be *uncontrollable*? How can you keep *everyone* busy and productive as a means of helping them cope with the uncertainty? Does cross-training people to do different jobs make sense?

9) Have you *really* taken the time to anticipate how the foreseeable changes may negatively impact people, morale, and productivity? Re-evaluate your progress as development moves ahead. Do you regularly talk with people at different levels in the organization, to understand how they see the current situation, and how changes might effect them? What are the *best-case*, *worse-case*, *most-likely case* implications for profitability of your organization based on the foreseeable changes? If your development effort takes twice as long and costs twice as much as you anticipated, will it still have made sense to do it?

10) Can you quickly pull together a core group of highly adaptive people and give them the authority to immediately implement necessary changes? Are you including the people whom others naturally follow, or tend to ask for advice?

11) Which people in your organization are best suited for working through situations involving uncertainty?

12) How can you acknowledge and deal with the sense of uncertainty people have who are most directly impacted by your development project? What can you do to recognize and acknowledge their anxiety, fears, or sense of loss in a compassionate manner?

13) Who in your own organization is most likely to resist the changes brought about by the elimination or scaling back of an existing service or product?

14) How do you intend to deal with malicious obedience or passive resistance resulting from the changing circumstances?

15) Will people be incentivized so they will derive some benefit they value highly?

16) How will you give people the time to grieve and emotionally adapt to the new situation? [Survivor Syndrome is real for many people; often the people who are most emotionally adversely affected by a major development project, a merger or an acquisition are the people who *survive*, and aren't fired or laid off.]

17) Have you looked for ways to compensate people for their losses either financially, or by giving them a greater sense of freedom and control over their immediate surroundings? Are you giving people current, accurate information about on-going changes and doing it relentlessly? How will the chain of command be configured to minimize rumors and anxiety in the organization?

18) Have you clearly communicated the scope of the reorganization that is planned, i.e., lay-offs/new hires, early retirements, transfers, reassignments?

19) How do you intend to recognize and acknowledge the contributions that people who are leaving have made to your organization? What can you do to help people find new jobs elsewhere? Has your organization made an effort to identify the highest risk employees, who are *least likely to be able to successfully adapt*? Have you developed a 'safety net' to avoid causing unnecessary human tragedies?

20) Have you done your best to help people understand how a brief period of uncertainty and discomfort can sometimes reveal a personal or organizational opportunity?

21) Have you asked colleagues who seem to be adapting well to the new changes, for their ideas and suggestions to share with others?

22) Have you created more flexible or relaxed temporary policies and procedures to help people cope with predictable periods of uncertainty? Can you identify tangible examples of how the organization is changing to help employees deal with the uncertainty, i.e., training programs, or incentives to help them stay focused and productive?

23) How can you rehearse people through the foreseeable changes that may predictably demoralize staff members who are powerless to protect themselves? What can you do to spare people from feeling like 'hunted animals?'

24) If you can't protect people, are you grouping necessary changes in a compassionate and understandable manner?

25) Can you create temporary roles, reporting relationships, and ad hoc work groups to help people get through the major periods of uncertainty?

26) Can you establish short term, easily achievable development goals for people to help them gain confidence? Can you anticipate where a greater level of communication is going to be important, or that breakdowns and gaps in communication are likely to occur, and devise compensating communication strategies to help them meet the challenges?

27) Can you find ways to keep people who aren't part of the business development effort feeling like they are still valued as an important part of the organization?

28) As part of your effort, can you set up a development adhocracy of people to be mindful of how *everyone* is coping with the changes, to keep channels of communication open, so people don't feel like they are intentionally being left out? How can you use the intranet to keep people informed?

29) Beyond the actively involved group, how can you keep a realistic working sense of how the development effort is fitting into the rest of the organization? Can you take the time to personally ask a cross-section of people throughout the organization how they think things are going, and seek feedback on how to improve the effort?

30) How can you encourage people to mindfully innovate, stretch themselves, experiment, and take intelligently calculated risks?

31) How can you get other people involved with the creative aspects of the development effort? How can you help people develop and use their creative abilities to make the business development effort a success?

32) How can you use the business development effort to encourage people to try doing things in new ways? Do you have an opportunity to set an example by coming up with workable solutions to problems that people have historically just had to live with?

33) How can you avoid pushing for answers on major decisions and closure to allow additional generations of thought to occur, when it might be beneficial to let people evaluate different scenarios, or search a little longer for the best answers and/or alternative solutions?

34) How can you avoid the risk of burning people out?

Independent Inventory Systems

For many companies, inventory costs, i.e., warehousing, financing of inventory, etc., used to account for 25% of the total cost of the goods which were sold. Today, better forecasting models, just-in-time production, overnight delivery companies, improved 'real time' channels of communication, and closer supplier-customer working relationships have reduced the amount of inventory many companies carry. The evolution of the internet and Long Tail and ability to get a geometrically larger number of things quickly and with relative ease has made the need to carry less time-sensitive inventory unnecessary

Bellwether's own research suggests that the most competitive companies have made significant efforts to control the size of their inventories as a means of preserving their liquidity. Put another way, the most competitive companies turn their inventory over more rapidly than their less competitive counterparts. A little time spent thinking about inventory management will lead one in the direction of believing that the cross-training of production workers will result in a more agile, albeit smaller workforce that is able to withstand economic disruptions that are likely to occur with growing frequency, due to the evolution of an equally skilled multinational workforce, climate change, political turbulence, polarizing economic trends, and an aging workforce in traditionally more well-educated and productive societies.

With those observations in mind, how will your answers to the following questions change in the months and years ahead?

1) How large do your inventories need to be? How can you anticipate demand from current or prospective customers more accurately? Should you be locating inventory closer to your major customers? Can you use drop shipping to avoid holding high-priced inventory in numerous locations?

2) Are you better off with a manual or computerized inventory system? Do you need a computerized system to get started if this is a new product or service? How long can you avoid the front-side expense of a computer system dedicated to managing inventory?

3) Which items in your inventory are routinely requested for production or repairs that demand your closest attention and control?

4) How much time, money and effort do you need to spend in order to maintain accurate inventory records? Can you rely on your billing records for inventory management purposes?

5) What part of your inventory generates the largest part of your profit?

6) How often do you review your lot sizes, safety stocks, the perishabilty or obsolescence of existing stock, and lead times with the objective of reducing inventory holding costs?

7) How do you take advantage of quantity discounts? How much sense does it make to carry extra stock considering storage, interest and handling charges?

8) How will the availability of supplies adversely effect your ability to compete or stay in business?

9) How can you foresee shortages and plan ahead to secure a steady supply?

10) Is it cost-effective for you to stop carrying high-priced inventory at numerous locations, and to ship it overnight to avoid inventory carrying costs?

11) How many times a year do you expect to turn over inventory of your high volume items?

12) From the time of request, how long does it take to put requested item(s) in the hands of your customer? (Can designated items automatically be put on a *fast track* to speed up response times? Who will have daily responsibility for overseeing the fast track part of your system?) How can you avoid fast tracking the more regularly requested parts of your inventory, to avoid the additional expense?

13) Who has the independent authority to request inventory items? What limits will they have on what items they can request?

14) What security risks would you be taking if you relaxed your processes for granting a wider range of people with authority to independently request inventory?

15) In terms of paperwork, how burdensome is your process to request an inventory item? (Do people circumvent or override your system on a regular basis because it is too slow? How often do they over-ride or circumvent it?)

16) How can you control shipping costs, i.e., rush charges and over-time, if you expand the number of people with the ability to independently request inventory items?

17) Do you have any organized processes for salvaging unused inventory on a regular basis?

18) Have you talked with customers to gain a realistic sense of short-term and long-term demand?

Drop Shipping and the growing viability of the Long Tail of e-commerce

With the evolution of e-commerce and the growth of the Long Tail as a viable marketing and sales channel, do you have an opportunity to carry a more diverse inventory of items that can be managed in a decentralized manner? What are the profit implications of managing a larger inventory in this manner?

Joint Ventures

Most joint ventures have a finite lifespan. Ultimately, what starts out as collaborative effort shifts as the relationship matures. This should be regarded as a normal evolution of the working relationship. With this in mind, both parties should have a clear perception of how the working relationship will conclude prior to entering into the joint venture. At pre-determined intervals, the idea of what each joint venture partner is getting from the working relationship should be discussed.

Some level of friction is normal in most working relationships. The higher the potential pay-off, the weaker the ties of the working relationship, the greater likelihood that the relationship will conclude sooner than it should, from a profit perspective. Suggestion: Resist the urge to pull back when signs of friction appear. That is the time when both parties should be leaning forward and looking to work through their differences.

Kaizen – Continuous Process Improvement – Development Of A Suggestion System

The nature of most businesses is to either improve or decline. How a business organizes itself, and its degree of receptivity to ideas about self-improvement is one of the clearer indicators of the long term vitality of an organization. The term Kaizen is the embodiment of the notion of continuous process improvement. Most organizations aligned with this approach have both formal and informal channels for ensuring proper consideration of ideas. Put another way, Kaizen represents a systematic approach to continuous process improvement. Suggestion Systems represent an essential part of a good Kaizen approach to continuous process improvement. A productive Suggestion System has identifiable traits:

1) Clear support by management, and open channels of communication
2) A sound, well-understood plan and policy
3) An adequate reward and recognition program
4) Careful follow-up and consideration of ideas
5) Timely acknowledgment and handling of suggestions
6) Good awareness of the Suggestion System inside the organization
7) Encouragement and help for employees in preparing ideas for consideration
8) Acknowledgment of ideas and recognition even for ideas that don't prove to be the best working solution at the time they are suggested.

Layout Plant / Office

1) What performance/productivity criteria and priorities are you using to determine layout? Do people understand how they will be evaluated [incentivized] and held accountable for making their space productive?

2) What is the best trade-off between being close to the customer or other operating divisions and other considerations related to layout? What self-imposed limitations/opportunities are you creating?

3) What storage or warehousing requirements are necessary for on-going activities? What are the geographic trade-offs of how your business is laid out? What inefficiencies and other trade-offs are you willing to live with?

4) Have the people who will be using the space been involved in the layout process from the beginning? How? Have outside vendors/suppliers been involved with designing the layout, based on their interaction with you, and their knowledge of other facilities, i.e., your competitors?

Legal Aspects Of Doing Business

1) Do your employees and/or other people representing you understand the legal constraints in terms of what they can do or say? Do they understand what standard of ethical behavior you expect from them, and how the personal and professional consequences of failing to meet those standards will impact them and the collective organization?

© Kerry O'Connor 1992, 1997, 1998, 2000, 2001, 2003, 2007

2) How much does your legal help know about your particular line of business and the following subjects as it relates to your business?

- Contractual Law
- Law Relating to Intellectual Property, Patents and Proprietary Rights
- Tax Law, State, Federal, and International
- Real Estate Law
- Bankruptcy Law
- Corporate and Securities Law
- Employment Law, State, Federal, and International

3) What is the current legal environment related to the sale and use of the product or services you are offering?

4) What can you proactively do to protect yourself and avoid lawsuits? Can you hire contract workers instead of employees?

<u>Location</u>

1) How will new locations be selected and managed? By employees, franchisees, distributors, contract managers?

2) What are the primary traits you are seeking in a new location? What secondary factors need to be considered? What are the cost considerations? Is the cost within your financial projections?

3) Does it make more sense to expand the size of your current location, or to expand to a new geographic location closer to existing, or prospective customers? If you're considering locating close to a major prospective customer, how can a guarantee of future business be tied to your decision to place a new facility near them? What form will the guarantee take? Have you discussed this with the current or prospective customer?

4) How does your quality of life or that of your employees enter into your decision regarding where to locate your new facility? What are the trade-offs, and how will they impact your ability to hire or retain valued employees? Besides anecdotal information, what are you basing your beliefs on?

5) What do you gain by being a leader versus a close/fast follower in picking new locations? What are the competitive advantages of the different options, compared side-by-side?

6) Should you organize your efforts by product or service line, market area, or access to natural resources, proximity to major clients?

7) Can you locate your office/production/retail facilities on-site where your customer does business, or lives? Related to your business, how has the internet/e-commerce impacted the importance of geographic locations?

Management

1) Who are the key people who will be responsible and accountable for making your endeavor a success? How committed are these people to the business opportunity you are considering? How much time, money, effort, and emotional energy are you willing to commit to make the endeavor a success? If you are in a large company do you have strong senior-level management support that you can turn to for help in adverse situations? Is anyone in senior management truly enthusiastic about the new opportunity? Realistically, how long and intensively is the core leadership team willing to be involved with the new venture?

2) Has anyone on the leadership team previously managed an effort similar to the one you are considering? Is there anyone who will assume the role of the business evangelist, or proverbial *keeper of the vision*? Is the person a serial business developer? Will the person stick around? How easy will it be to find someone to replace the project leader?

3) How strong will your management team be in the following areas?

- Sales, Marketing and Public Relations
- Management & Strategic Development Of Product and Services
- Law and Taxes
- E-commerce
- Operations/Production/Service Delivery
- Financial Management
- Human Resources

4) How would you describe the individual skills of the management team in the following areas?

- Problem Solving – raw intelligence, flexibility, energy and perseverance
- Communication / Information Technology
- Decision-Making
- Project Management
- Negotiating
- Managing Staff
- Managing Outside Professionals and Supplier Relationships
- Human Resource Administration
- Crisis Management

5) How have managerial roles and responsibilities been clearly defined?

6) How long will it take to assemble the key members of the management team? What are you estimating it will cost you in money, time, and effort to assemble your core management team?

7) Is customer segmentation and specialization necessary to grow the business to meet your financial objectives? If this is the case, how will your priorities and staffing reflect it?

8) Currently, which of your rivals represents the largest competitive threat to your new venture? Are they smaller or larger competitors? Realistically, how would you describe your competition's managerial strengths? How do they compare with those of your management team? Have you considered acquiring your most well-managed competitor?

9) Are new, or supposedly weaker or less well-managed competitors succeeding with new approaches you thought couldn't work? What traits or attributes are enabling them to succeed in spite of their managerial shortcomings?

10) Related to your ability to assign, develop, or recruit the managerial talent you'll need, how perishable is the opportunity you're evaluating?

11) What external competitive factors make the opportunity worth pursuing? Do changes in management at a rival company offer you the chance to recruit valuable employees, who will significantly improve your competitive position?

12) Does your management team agree on your market entry strategy?

13) Does your management team agree on an exit strategy? [Have you developed several different scenarios?] What are the risks, rewards and trade-offs? What is the salvage value at different stages of development?

14) What level of customer service is required to deal with the aftermarket related to this product or service? Who needs to be part of your start-up team as a result?

15) Do any of your top managers have experience successfully selling your new product or service? How will customers buy your services or products? How long will it take them to make a purchase decision? How intensively will your management team be involved with the sales process?

16) Who on the management team will be responsible for approving major and minor expenditures? How much experience do they have managing and protecting cash flows and financial reserves in new ventures?

17) What trade-offs are you willing to make in your decision to pursue your new opportunity? What other opportunities are you ignoring? What's it going to cost you short term or long term?

18) How comfortable are the key people at dealing with the uncertainty involved with developing of new products, services or retail locations?

19) How much importance do other core team members tie to the success of the new business? How dedicated are they? Do they have anything to lose? What do they have to gain?

20) Do people outside of the core team know what you need from them in order to succeed? Will they cooperate? Can they provide the needed assistance in a timely manner?

21) If you're considering developing a new product or service, as an organization, are you willing to abandon the project if you discover unfavorable information prior to your 'live' public start date? Who will make the *kill* decision?

22) How will your managers be evaluated and be held responsible for working together? Do people have a clear idea of what is expected of them? Do they understand how other people are counting on them?

23) Does the existing management team share a common perception of how the organization will value the new service or product, and where it 'fits in'?

Managerial Staffing

1) What kind of skills and experience does the person you're evaluating have related to:

Administration/Management

- Problem solving – Raw intelligence, resourcefulness/ability to improvise, energy, stamina and perseverance
- Communication skills – Interpersonal day-to-day inside the company & going on sales calls when needed, dealing with the investor community, customer relations management, and public relations – dealing with the trade media
- Decision-Making/Decisiveness
- Project Management – Leadership, team building skills, scheduling, experience producing final deliverables
- Negotiating – Experience and relevant understanding of the objectives & related factors
- Managing Employees – Short term and long term ability to motivate people
- Managing Outside Professionals, i.e., Consultants or Contract Employees
- Human Resource Administration – Ability to understand the legal ramifications of different decisions
- Crisis Management – Resilience and ability to respond appropriately in adverse situations

- International experience/understanding – Direct understanding of the cultural, regulatory and political realities in relevant geographic areas of the company's business interests
- Stress Resistance & Stamina – Intellectual ruggedness

Law and Taxes
- Basic Business Law, State, Federal, Relevant Multinational
- Contract Law, National and Relevant Multinational
- Law Relating to Intellectual Property, Patents, Proprietary Rights
        And Licensing Agreements
- Tax Law, State, Federal, and Multinational
- Real Estate Law
- Bankruptcy Law
- Corporate and Securities Law
- Employment Law, State, Federal, and Relevant Multinational

Marketing, Sales, Strategic Planning, e-commerce
- Strategic Planning
- Marketing
- Market Development
- Sales
- E-commerce
- Market Research and Analysis
- Marketing Forecasting and Planning
- Product and/or Service Pricing
- Sales Management and Staffing
- Direct Selling and Negotiation
- Monitoring the Delivery of Service and Customer Satisfaction
- Channel Marketing & Distribution Management
- Product/Service Marketing & Advertising Management
- New Product/Service Planning, Development, and Introduction
- E-commerce Development

Operations/Production/Service Delivery
- Manufacturing/Service Management
- Inventory/Staff Management
- Cost Analysis and Control
- Quality Control

- Production & Operating Management
- Production Scheduling and Process Flow Management
- Purchasing Versus Leasing
- Trouble-Shooting
- Distribution & Logistics Management

Finance
- Raising Capital
- Managing Cash Flow
- Credit and Collection Management
- Short-term Financing Alternatives
- Public and Private Offerings
- Bookkeeping Accounting and Control
- Developing Financial-Reporting Information Systems
- Financial Analysis
- Forecasting/Regression Analysis
- Strategic Alliances, Licensing Arrangements, Joint Ventures

Human Resources
- Recruiting and Staffing
- Employee Termination and Lay-Offs
- Outsourcing; Contractual Workers
- Managerial Staff Assessment, Development & Training
- Team-Building

2) How important is it to have a full range of managerial talent on staff before deciding to move ahead? How can you compensate for short-comings in managerial staffing?

3) What is the individual level of commitment of the most important people to stay with the project for a predefined period of time, i.e., two years?

4) What is the person's long-term suitability for the job the person is being considered for? Will the person continue to grow as the requirements of the job grow? For how long? Is the person more entrepreneurial, or more managerial/administrative?

5) Who is going to be included in selecting the managerial staff? Will direct reports to the position being filled have the opportunity to interview candidates for the position?

6) What is the person's management style: group consensus, autocratic, a good delegator, charismatic, command and control?

Marketing Research

1) Who currently offers similar products or services for sale? What has your competition's experience been selling the product or service?

2) How in-depth and current is your top marketing and sales manager's knowledge of your major competitor's behavior and activities related to marketing and the selling of the product or service? [Are you relying on anecdotal information?]

3) How can you get the marketing research staff involved to realistically evaluate the market potential of the new product or service before you invest a lot of time and money?

4) Has the marketing research staff visited with, or spoken in-depth, with at least three organizations who *already* have experience working with, and/or selling the new product or service?

5) Has the marketing research staff visited with, or spoken in-depth, with at least three organizations who are solid *prospective* customers for this product or service, with the objective of finding out how strong their interest is in *actually* buying the new product or using the new service?

6) How long will it take to develop a new product or service product to the level of the what your competitor is selling? What were the pitfalls your competition initially encountered in their early efforts to see the product or service? Would they get into this business if they weren't already in it? What would they do differently if they were to start over again?

7) What do your prospective customers value most in your new product or service? Is it price, location, quality, speed, reliability & durability, safety, prestige, user experience, or customer support?

8) Is your new product or service unique? Would uniqueness be valued by your prospective customers or end users? Will the new product or service be sold as a commodity or built to universal standards? If uniqueness or differentiation is important, from a competitive perspective, how long will your customers be willing to pay a premium? Does this product or service have a life cycle in terms of how long prospective customers intend to keep buying or using it? Realistically, what is the life cycle of the new product or service, and what opportunities exist to develop additional products or services if the new product or service you are considering developing turns out to be a success?

9) How can you test market your new product or service prior to full scale implementation?

10) Based on research, who should be part of the core development team? Do the people who represent your core development team have the individual talents needed to make this project a success? Have they ever worked together?

11) What <u>organizational</u> traits or attributes do you believe could help or hurt you? How can you test your beliefs, i.e., by having an independent research organization gather a core sampling from potential customers to see how important the product or [customer] service characteristics are to them?

12) Have you talked with your potential customers to learn why they are frustrated with their current supplier, and asked why they would switch and buy from you?

13) What are the three most important reasons why customers currently buy this product or service?

13) How do you plan to track customer satisfaction and spot customer service problems?

14) Can you conduct split-run tests to assess what prospective customers regard as the key attributes of the product or service?

Marketing And Sales

1) Do you currently sell this product or service? How are you teaching the sales and marketing communications staff to sell it? How are you getting them involved at the earliest stages of development?

2) What are the unique characteristics of your product or service?

3) Does anyone on your staff have experience selling this product or service? How are you encouraging them and supporting their efforts to develop marketing and sales strategies, and go out and sell the product or service?

4) Are people on the marketing & sales staff personally enthusiastic about the opportunity to sell the product or service? Do they have any immediate opportunities to sell the product or service? Working with your marketing and sales people, how can you assess the market potential of the product or service before making a major commitment? What formal and informal, traditional and non-traditional methods can you use to evaluate the sales potential of the product or service?

5) Have you challenged the marketing and sales staff to come up with breakthrough ideas regarding how to market or sell the product? Can you allocate an adequate level of sales support to your new product or service to make it successful?

6) How much attention will the new product or service take away from existing products and services, and the related cash flow?

7) Who on the marketing & sales staff are most well-suited to working on the new product or service? Does the new product or service represent an opportunity for members of your staff who badly need a challenge? How can you give the people a sense of ownership?

8) How do the ecommerce & wireless & digital, inside telephone sales, and televideo-conferencing fit into the sales & marketing communications mix, if at all?

9) Who is responsible and who else should also be involved developing the initial draft of the marketing plan and who is responsible for approving the final *marketing plan*? Who is responsible and who should also be involved developing the *sales strategy*?

10) Ultimately, who is responsible for synthesizing the various ideas and putting together a solid marketing and sales effort? How much does the person know about the following subjects, and how they inter-relate on a day-to-day basis:

> Market Research and Analysis
> Marketing & Sales Forecasting and Planning
> Product and/or Service Pricing
> Sales Management and Staffing
> Direct Selling and Negotiation
> E-commerce
> Monitoring the Delivery of Products and Services and
> Customer Satisfaction
> Distribution Management
> Product/Service Management
> New Product/Service Planning, Development, and Introduction?

11) Have you developed realistic monthly, quarterly and annual sales projections for this product or service? Do you have enough sales staff to meet your projections? Will part of the sales staff be dedicated exclusively to selling this product or service?

12) Who stands to benefit the most if the new product or service succeeds? Who stands to benefit most if the new product or service fails? How can you neutralize people who want to see the new product or service fail?

13) Are your marketing assumptions and sales projections consistent with those developed by other people in the organization, i.e., operations' planning, finance? If your projections are significantly different from those of other people, have you talked with the others to figure out why? How have you resolved any differences?

14) What are your throughput requirements for the new product or service? How close are your sales projections to financial break-even?

15) What contingency plans have you developed in the event the new product or service proves more successful, or less successful, than anticipated?

16) How often will you track and measure and evaluate the results of your efforts?

17) Are there bellwether customers who influence the buying patterns of other customers, who should be targeted first? How can the marketing and sales staff get early and on-going feedback from these influential potential customers?

18) What seasonal or cyclical aspects or buying patterns of customers should be kept in mind?

19) What have you done to understand the buying patterns of your most important prospective customers?

20) Do you know who the various participants [stakeholders and scorekeepers] are in the selection or procurement process at your prospective customer, and do you understand their different specific technical and economic interests?

21) What kind of incentives are you giving the sales and marketing staffs? Is the incentive based on the collective performance of the group, on individual performance, or some combination of both group and individual performance? Is there a commonly accepted industry standard for how people are incentivized that people are used to?

22) Have you structured your project to quickly reward people who show initiative that have just joined your organization, so they don't become discouraged and leave?

23) How do you plan to divide sales territories, i.e., geographically, size of account?

24) What kind of on-going sales training are you giving people? Will new sales staff be assigned to someone who knows the new product or service for a defined period of time, i.e., 30 days or six months?

25) Do the sales and marketing staffs believe there are realistically enough potential customers who are willing to buy the product or service within a given period of time, to make it a success?

26) When will your sales people receive their commission from a sale, e.g., at the time you receive payment, as a percentage drawn against the life of the contract, or for a finite period of time?

27) What is your policy on the payment of commissions after the sales person leaves the company?

28) Can your sales staff answer the following questions:

- What is your company's legal operating structure, i.e., a 'C' corporation, Sub-Chapter S, a limited liability partnership? If the company is closely held, (with fewer than 30 shareholders), who are the principal investors/owners?
- Does your company or management team's history of achievement and reputation indicate leadership, innovation, effectiveness, results, effective management, sound budgeting and effective planning, and fulfillment of customer expectations?
- How do the traits of your organization compare with those with other suppliers?
- Does your prospective customer currently buy the new product or service from other suppliers? Do they need to buy it to stay in business?

- Does your company offer a product or service that solves a clearly identifiable problem for the prospective customer? Can you offer tangible examples?
- How would the prospective customer's business fit into your company's current mix of clients, i.e., would they be a big, important customer, would they be ignored because they are too small?
- What can the prospective client expect in the form of customer support?
- What are your plans for growth? How long do you intend to continue providing customer support for this product or service?

Materials Management

1) Does it make sense to have a more vertically or horizontally integrated materials management structure? What other organizations in related businesses have demonstrated long-term success at managing materials, using either a more or less horizontally or vertically integrated structure?

2) How are you selecting, evaluating, and supporting your suppliers? How well do you communicate? Are you giving them adequate lead times and constructive feedback?

3) Can you take advantage of leverage associated with more centralized buying? What are the trade-offs between long-term, short-term, or exclusivity – sole source of supply contracts?

4) Does it make sense to add distribution centers and position inventory to be closer to customers? Would such a move translate into a meaningful tangible benefit to you or for your customer?

5) How often do you formally evaluate whether your inventories and other production levels are too low or too high? Do your suppliers have excess capacity? How often do your customers work at full capacity, consume your inventory, and create significant short term demands on your production system?

6) What are your best options for reducing inventory?

7) How can you directly tie materials management to competitive priorities and production realities? Who are the process stakeholders who should be directly involved with establishing production schedules, directly or indirectly impacting materials management?

8) Can you subcontract additional production? How will subcontracting production impact your space requirements and materials management activities?

9) How are you using just-in-time delivery scheduling? How does it impact materials management?

10) What are you doing to eliminate warehousing, and move to same day turnarounds if you are using a hub and spoke materials management system?

11) What is the maximum acceptable length of time for keeping an item in inventory?

12) How much valuable space are you using to store obsolete materials? How often do you check inventory?

Materials / Service Planning (MP/SP)

1) What information is available from MP/SP systems that could help you manage materials/services better? Have you visited, or spoken in-depth, with at least three non-competing businesses with MP/SP systems to learn how they manage MP/SP?

2) How is a formal MP/SP system appropriate for your organization?
Who will benefit the most from the new MP/SP system, and how should they be involved with the planning and selection process?

3) How much will it cost in terms of time (disruption), money, and effort, will it be for you to implement an MP/SP system? What specific things can you do to minimize your tangible and intangible expenses?

4) How can you use MP to manage non-manufacturing inventories?

5) Do people with expertise in MP/SP in one part of your organization constructively share their knowledge with people in other parts of your organization on a regular basis? What other parts of the organization would benefit from having more open channels of communication with them?

New Technologies

1) What new technologies could quickly improve the productivity of your employees in a measurable way? In what ways will the new technology and/or equipment be different? What new skills and knowledge will your people need? Which members of your organization will need it? When will they need it to use the new technology effectively? How will people need to adjust their attitudes to make the adoption of the new technology successful? How long will the new technology be considered state-of-the-art? If the new technologies aren't yet proven or cost-effective, how are you planning to take advantage of them when the price comes down, or the technology sufficiently improves to justify your expenditure/investment?

2) In the foreseeable future, how will new technologies increase productivity or reduce your costs, and improve your ability to bring new products or services to market?

3) How can low-cost/technology & automation help you achieve the benefits of standardization enabling long production runs, and minimizing disruptions to other parts of your organization?

4) Does dedicated or programmable/technology/automation make sense for a particular situation? Have you visited other organizations where the new technology you're considering incorporating into your business is being used with quantifiable success?

5) Are you strenuously avoiding becoming an alpha site for an unproven technology?

6) What is the productive life span of the new equipment? Can it be easily and cost-effectively updated? Is the technology compatible with commonly accepted industry standards? Will you be captive to one supplier?

7) Can economies of scale derived from using the new technology give you a competitive advantage? For how long? How do you intend to achieve these economies of scale? Whose technical support do you need?

8) How will the introduction of this new technology effect your staffing levels? Is the new technology you are considering worth the time and disruption it will cause? How much of a factor is it to your top producers to have access to state of the art equipment? Will they leave if they don't get it? Have they left other organizations in the past for similar reasons?

Operations as a Competitive Resource

1) How are you making your operations/staffing a more competitive resource? Have you asked for ideas from your own people?

2) How are your competitors using operations/service staffing to be more competitive? Have you talked with customers who buy from both you and your competitor of you to get feedback from them? Who else can you talk with? Do you regularly solicit honest feedback from your current customers, and from prospective customers?

3) How are you using operations to drive new product or service development?

4) How do you monitor operations for problems and opportunities? What are you doing to avoid becoming complacent about how you operate your business?

5) What are your high-leverage opportunities for improving operations that will produce a long-term competitive advantage?

6) Have you identified 3 non-competing organizations with similar lines of business or organizational structure that you can share best practices with, along with *lessons learned* about what to avoid?

7) How often do you visit innovative, non-competing operating facilities, *including* other facilities seemingly totally unrelated to your line of work, to get new ideas? When you go on these site visits, do you take different employees who have a stake in operations to get different perspectives?

8) Do your current suppliers clearly understand that you hope and expect they will regularly bring you new ideas and offer suggestions about how you can improve operations?

9) What are the industry norms for operating expense ratios? If your operating expense ratios are competitively favorable, how does it motivate or stifle your decision to develop and introduce new products or services?

10) What is your total operating expense as a percentage of gross revenue? Do your competitors evaluate operating costs the same way you do? Are they bound by the same financial constraints, i.e., are they publicly or privately owned?

11) As a whole, and by department, what is the salary and wage expense ratio? How are the ratios likely to change during the next 6 – 12 months? As a whole, and by department, what are the overtime and outsourcing expenses as a percentage of total salaries and wages?

12) What is the expense of each department as a total percentage of costs?

13) What is the operating productivity for:

- Distribution – shipping, drop-shipping, emailing, stops per driver per day?
- Manufacturing
- Service delivery outbound (including site management)
- Warehouse – pick/pack per full time equivalent (FTE) per day?
- Customer Service – orders per customer service representative (CSR) per day?
- Billing – total claims collected per FTE per day?
- Sales
- Marketing, PR, promotion

14) What opportunities exist to consolidate or outsource operating activities?

15) Where can cross-training reduce the need for additional operating staff, or limit the adverse effects of absenteeism? How can cross-training make you more competitive and enable you to seek new business opportunities you would otherwise couldn't pursue?

16) How can outsourcing be utilized to make operations more profitable, less stressful, or help you balance work flows more easily?

17) How can your b*est demonstrated operating practices* be standardized?

18) Can your operating processes be mapped out to identify down cycles, gaps and inefficiencies that can be managed to reduce [overtime] staffing?

19) How can other departments, i.e., sales & marketing work with operations to support staff efforts to improve profitability?

20) How much does the person responsible for operations know about the following areas:

- Manufacturing/Service Management
- Inventory/Staff Planning & Management
- Cost Analysis and Cost Control
- Quality Control
- Production/Staff Scheduling and Flow
- Financial Management, i.e., Purchasing Versus Leasing
- Sales and Marketing
- Investor Relations
- Human Resources
- Customer Service & Customer Relationship Management

People

1) What traits or attributes should the people have who are likely to be most capable of helping you achieve your growth objectives during the *start-up phase*?
2) What traits or attributes should the people have who are likely to be most capable of helping you grow the business *mid-term*, or *long term*?
3) Of the people you are considering hiring, who has the best understanding of the requirements of the job? What are the person's greatest strengths? What weaknesses does the person have, and how can you compensate for them?
4) Of the people you are evaluating, who has the strongest working relationships with your staff and/or distribution channel marketing partners?
5) Who has the most experience on your staff bringing new products/services to market?
6) Who has the best understanding of current clients/customers and why some things may be different than how they appear?
7) How intellectually rugged and agile in their thinking are the different people you are considering?
8) Does the person have the emotional stamina and willingness to see the job through? How does the person respond to pressure?
9) How willing are the different people to adapt to new circumstances and situations?
10) How resilient are the different people you are considering at dealing with un-anticipated changes, setbacks, and other forms of adversity?
11) To what extent do the various people you are considering want the new product or service to succeed?

12) If the person has reservations about how successful a new product or service will be, is it possible the person has knowledge you don't, that could be valuable; can you find out why the person has concerns?

13) How realistically optimistic are the various people you are considering to have lead the development effort about being able to make the new product(s) or service(s) a success?

14) How well do the different people you are evaluating understand the past operating dynamics of your business and how it fits into the marketplace? Do they understand how some of the operating dynamics are be likely to change in the near future?

15) Is the person who you believe is the best person for the job willing to relocate?

16) Are the people comprising the core development team willing to be cross-trained\ to perform different job duties, to at least gain a greater appreciation for other business activities on which the success of the business development effort depends?

17) On a person-by-person basis, how well does the person take direction? How much coaching or direction will the person need to reach the level of effectiveness you envision? Is the person self-motivated to improve themselves? How have they demonstrated that trait or attribute in the past?

Pricing

1) Who will establish pricing guidelines? Who will have the authority to make exceptions?

2) What pricing methods are you using to establish pricing for your new product or service?

3) Are your pricing methodologies consistent with contractual standards within your business segment? How are they different regionally, nationally, or internationally?

4) Will your pricing policies take into consideration that it is customary for people and organizations in different parts of the world to take widely varying lengths of time to pay their bills?

5) How elastic is your pricing? What external real or perceived barriers exist to prevent you from raising prices?

6) What is the highest price you can charge for your product or service? How do you know?

7) To what extent is price a determining factor in your customer's decision to use your product/service and/or that of your competition?

8) How long are you guaranteeing the price you are currently quoting or offering, 30 days, 90 days?

9) How does your pricing compare with that of your competition? What is your competition's history of pricing their products or services?

10) How can you use pricing to gain a competitive advantage, and how long do you anticipate your advantage will last?

11) How much flexibility do you have in pricing? To what extent are you willing to offer discounts in exchange for long-term contracts? What about offering a discount in exchange for prompt payment, i.e., within 10 or 30 days?

12) What percentage of total payment do you expect to receive within 30 days of signing an initial contract?

13) If you're billing for a service, are you billing at the beginning or end of the month?

14) Do you bill for products when shipped, or at the end of the month?

15) Are you willing to trade off cash up-front in exchange for equity?

16) Are you willing or able to factor receivables?

17) Are you going to use a bundled, or an a la carte, pricing methodology?

18) Will you offer off-peak pricing? How are you going to pass through rush charges or over-time costs?

Process Design / Process Mapping

1) What methods will you use to produce, market and distribute/deliver your product or service?

2) How do capital requirements, equipment and staffing fit into the process design?

3) What alternative production processes or staffing arrangements should be considered which could, or might be able to, meet your needs?

4) How capital intensive will your production process be? How does financing or refinancing fit into the process design so cost-effective alternatives can be built into the process design?

5) How flexible should your staff be in terms of their respective skill sets and/or their ability to think outside of their traditional scope of expertise in order to keep the project moving, and increase the overall chances of success? How willing are people to get outside of their comfort zones? Can you think of specific situations where people involved with the development effort have demonstrated that ability in the past?

6) How necessary is it for the jobs to be specialized or cross-functional? Will people be formally cross-trained to perform more than one job?

7) How vertically integrated will your product line or service range be, and how will this influence how you design your work processes?

8) Related to the process design of how you produce and deliver your products or services, how much are you involving your customer and/or your outside partner(s), if your project is part of a joint venture or a strategic alliance?

9) What other parts of your organization need to be involved in the early stages with changes to the design of operating processes, i.e., other divisions, information services, billing & finance, R&D, logistics, customer service, sales and marketing?
10) What parts of other organizations, i.e., suppliers, should, or need to be involved in determining the design of your operating processes? Do they have legal constraints or limitations in terms of knowledge sharing of which you need to be aware?

Production / Work Scheduling

1) How do your competitive priorities determine your priorities involving production/service delivery scheduling? Is there an understanding and agreement inside your organization by all the people [stakeholders] who are directly involved? How are responsibilities divided?
2) What can you do to get better estimates of production flows and capacity requirements to schedule production more effectively? Who is directly accountable for incrementally and systematically improving the production system?
3) How closely does your final production schedule resemble your initial production plan? When is the best time to involve the various production stakeholders with production scheduling?
4) How can you take advantage of just-in-time scheduling and production/staffing? How can cross-training of employees make scheduling and staffing less stressful?
5) Who will be indirectly impacted by your production schedule and kept informed about how you are actually working to plan? Who is directly responsible for on-going communication regarding production scheduling/staffing, and communicating with stakeholders when there are changes in production?

Product / Service Planning -- Assigning Priorities

1) Does your new or existing product or service represent a core business opportunity?
2) How does this product or service fit into your competitive priorities?
3) At what stage do you intend to enter and exit the market during the product or service life cycle?
4) Are you willing to sell, liquidate, or cannibalize this product/service or business if it fails to meet your objectives? Are you keeping a rough approximation of what the salvage value of the capital equipment and total cost of various kill fees will be if you decide to shut down the project?
5) What criteria are you using to determine when you will add or drop products or services? What level of support do you intend to provide after a product or service is no longer available?

6) To what extent will the business opportunity siphon off managerial attention from other more important projects or services? How will the assignment of priorities reflect an emphasis on your highest value projects, while being mindful not to starve major sources of future cash flow?

7) What impact will this new product or service have on other existing operations? Will it complement them, represent a promising new source of sustainable revenue, or serve as an interesting distraction?

8) What sales volume are you planning for this product or service to have in 2 years? What percentage of your business's total sales do you envision coming from this product or service in four years? What level of staffing and financial resources will be required? Are you personally willing to make the commitment to stay with the project through to completion? If not, who will replace you?

Production and Staffing

1) Do the people on whom you are depending understand your production goals and how their direct or indirect assistance or involvement may or will be required? What traits or attributes do these people have?

2) Have you taken the time to provide your production/operating/sales staff with an overview of how production and other organizational jobs are interdependent, and how people rely on one another?

3) How can you anticipate and avoid 'surprises' in meeting your production goals? Can you identify early warning signs, which automatically change production processes and staffing? How closely integrated is your business development, marketing and sales strategy, with your production plan?

4) How can you manage production and staffing to reduce operating costs, i.e., over-time labor costs, employee turnover, special deliveries, rush charges, etc.?

5) Do you need rigid [command and control] work-force staffing and production, or would a flexible work-force arrangement give you better results?

6) Can you use subcontracting to achieve short-term production increases and avoid overtime and/or seasonal hiring?

7) What is the minimum level of training employees require to perform their jobs in a consistently competent manner?

8) How can you use work teams to improve quality, reduce turnover, and improve morale?

9) Can some parts of your production requiring simple repetitive tasks be out-sourced to sheltered workshops, i.e., bulk mailings, the manual entering of basic repetitive information into computers, etc.?

10) Can part or all of your production [and related staffing] be subcontracted or outsourced to lower cost or more efficient labor markets?

Project Scheduling

1) How can you anticipate and avoid expensive project delays?

2) Which time sensitive activities in your project have to be managed most tightly during the project to stay on schedule and on time? Can parts of the project be started sooner to create a buffer or managed in a parallel process with others to stay on track? What scheduling methods will improve your ability to control or reduce costs and provide better customer service?

3) How may scarce resources threaten your ability to keep the project moving? Have you developed a contingency plan? How and when do you plan to allocate resources differently in the future?

4) How can you include foreseeable delays and uncertainty in the time estimates for various production activities in the scheduling process?

5) Who will have on-site, day-to-day direct operating responsibility and authority for making sure the project achieves its goals? To what extent are you empowering people on-site to make decisions that will keep the project on schedule?

Quality Management

1) How will your customers measure the quality of your work? Do different customers measure quality differently? Can you gain a competitive advantage by defining quality in an acceptable manner to customers, that your competitors will find difficult to match? Can you establish the standards of measurement?

2) How can you demonstrate the quality of your product or service to current and prospective customers in a meaningful and memorable way?

3) How can technological advances help you improve quality and profitability? Will in-sourcing or out-sourcing part of your work improve the quality? Can you demonstrate quality that will clearly be seen as value-added by current or prospective customers?

4) How long will you be able to maintain your quality advantage? Will the quality-driven portion of the market be large enough or be interested in purchasing your product long enough to provide adequate returns on your investment? How expensive will it be for you to achieve an acceptable level of quality? Can you pass the additional cost through to your customers? Will they pay for it? Have you asked them?

5) Do you understand the economic implications for pricing and profits of new technology or other alternatives for improving quality?

6) How can you preempt your competitors by taking advantage of new quality-related improvements in technology? How long will it take for your quality-related advantage to be recognized by current or prospective customers?

7) How long will your quality-related advantage last, based on the new or improved technology? Can you, or anyone, implement the technology and prove its benefits rapidly enough to meet the time-to-market requirements in order to fully exploit the opportunity?

8) What are the current lead times for changes in technology or service delivery [research & development, acquisition, or gaining regulatory approval, etc.] needed to significantly improve quality or increase capacity?

9) How do customers perceive the quality of your product or service? Are you providing [and paying for] additional benefits the customer does or doesn't value?

10) How do current or prospective customers, in their own words, define quality in your product or service?

11) Is the perception of quality by your customers a clearly defined, heavily-weighted factor related to their purchase decision?

12) Can you profitably achieve a consistent, acceptable level of quality?

13) How are you involving your employees, i.e., sales and marketing, finance, research & development, suppliers and customers in your quality improvement efforts?

14) What factors in your operating system are likely to cause your biggest quality problems? Who will be directly responsible for dealing with those problems? Will the person or people responsible for fixing the quality problems be assigned to the effort long enough to do an adequate job? Will they have the authority (including a budget) to get the job done? Will they have the clearly understood support of senior management?

15) What quality-assurance role does your operating staff see itself playing related to customer service? How will they have control over the product they produce, or the service they provide?

16) What specific organization-wide quality-related standards of service do you have?

17) What are the most important quality-related traits sought by your customers? What important quality-related criteria do you need to meet to satisfy your customers?

18) How can you improve the quality of your product or service in the short-term?

19) What regular quality-related feedback can you seek from your customers?

20) How do you identify mistakes and related expenses resulting from poor quality work?

21) Are you encouraging your suppliers to implement quality control methods you can verify?

22) How do your training efforts reflect your beliefs and expectations related to quality?

23) What on-going education do you provide for people who are responsible for the quality of the products or services you sell, i.e., in-service training/education, visits to customers, visits to end users of your product or services? Does it makes sense to seek quality-related accreditations, etc.?

24) Do you plan to teach all your employees the concepts of quality improvement? Are the appropriate employees receiving training?

25) Are you providing operational definitions of the quality requirements for each job that even temporary employees can quickly understand? Do the appropriate people (including temporary workers) understand what role they play in producing the level of quality being sought?

26) Are you going to provide on-going training with the objective of having all your employees fully understand their roles in improving quality six months or a year from now? How are you teaching people to identify and eliminate the recurring sources of problems, mistakes, and defects in quality on their own?

27) Are you requiring your supervisors to gain a working knowledge of the key aspects of quality improvement such as statistical process control in order to help the people working under their direction?

28) Are you developing a system to monitor quality and identify the sources of problems that can be easily understood? Are you building a feedback system that helps employees know when to take action?

29) How are you encouraging quality-related communication between employees, departments, customers and suppliers?

30) Are competitors in other parts of the country or world defining quality differently? What can you learn from them?

Research and Development (R&D)

1) How often do you have to introduce new services, products, product extensions or upgrades in order to meet your growth projections?

2) How are R&D activities integrated into your overall business activities? How difficult is it to 'field test' new products or services? What are the advantages and disadvantages of limited public disclosure?

3) Approximately what percentage of your R&D budget should be spent on developing proprietary products or services, and what percentage should be spent doing knock-offs or licensing technologies and methodologies developed by other people and organizations?

4) Are your R&D activities externally driven by customer requests for new products or services? Are your customers most likely to approach you or your competition when it comes to developing new products or services? Do your suppliers bring you their new product or service ideas first, or do they take it to your competitors because they assume you won't be interested, based on prior experience?

5) To what extent can R&D working cooperatively with your sales and marketing staff enable you to adapt your existing products or services for use in new markets?

6) How do your competitors organize their R&D activities? What percent of their total budget is allocated to research and development?

7) What opportunities exist to collaborate with other organizations on R&D activities as a means of reducing your time-to-market?

8) How do you intend to field test your products or services? Do you intend to field test your products or services in different regions of the world, or a variety of different conditions?

9) How willing are your current customers to act as an alpha site, to test your new products or services?

10) Do you have the opportunity to place members of your R&D staff on-site to work with the R&D staff of your customers, to make sure your company's products or services are an integral part of what your customers need to launch *their* new products or services?

11) What total percentage of gross revenue from the new product or service do you expect to be derived from sales inside your originating country versus other parts of the world?

12) Does it make sense to organize your R&D activities to focus on developing multinationally scalable products or services?

13) How are your R&D and marketing activities linked [across geographic regions] so the products or services being developed can be more successfully marketed, require less end-user modification, and improve the ROI on both your R&D activities and your sales and marketing communications activities?

Staff Incentives

1) What is the objective of offering incentives:

- to increase sales efforts
- to motivate operations to increase production
- to improve the quality of the work being produced
- to more successfully recruit highly talented people
- to retain your most highly valued people
- to reduce absenteeism or turnover

2) What kind of incentives are people most interested in, i.e., cash bonuses, time off, longer term financial incentives including stock options, use of a company car, being able to work at home or off-site, tuition reimbursement? How do you know? Can you offer employees different incentives using a cafeteria-style model?

3) What criteria will be used to establish the basis for the incentives? Will it be consistent with other parts of the organization? If the answer is no, are there sufficient reasons to justify making an exception in the situation being considered?

4) What incentives can be offered to people in similar situations or jobs comparable to those offered at competing organizations? Are there commonly accepted incentives in your industry for some employees, i.e., sales staff, or senior executives?

5) If part of the compensation will be in the form of stock options:

- how will the options be valued if the stock isn't publicly traded?
- how rapidly will the options vest, i.e., what percentage will vest after the first year?
- do the options become fully vested in the event of a takeover or merger?
- from date of issue, when will the options expire?

6) As the related incentives increase in financial value, will employees be expected to sign non-compete, or non-disclosure agreements that might have at least a short-term, i.e., 18 months, on their job prospects in the future?

7) Do you intend to provide spot bonuses or other rewards for both employees and non-employees who bring you business? How do you intend to define a person's role in winning new business to justify paying a bonus? Will it be on a 'you-win we-win' basis or some other method?

8) Do you intend to offer incentives to everyone in your organization? Will you alienate employees who aren't offered incentives? How will an incentive system that favors one group of employees over another effect morale?

<u>Strategy and Tactics</u>

1) What is your strategy for moving from your present market position into a more favorable position? Have you put your strategy in writing in the form of a strategic plan? Can you establish a timetable and specific objectives for reaching your interim goals? How do other people inside your company, joint-venture partners, sources of funding need to be made aware of your intentions, and to be supportive?

2) How will your product or service positioning in the marketplace support your strategy? Does your strategy emphasize unique product or service attributes, i.e., superior quality, time-saving, a reduction in end user operating costs, competitively superior customer service, better pricing, greater operating flexibility, improved customer satisfaction, or a technological breakthrough? How does your positioning and strategy reflect the competitive advantage you will be delivering in the marketplace?

3) How will the business, service or product be comparatively and competitively positioned against the rest of the market? How easy is it to implement your strategy? How do you intend to capitalize on your strategic advantage? Realistically, how long do you expect your strategic advantage to last, and how do you intend to capitalize on your strategy – what additional strategic maneuvering do you have planned?

4) How do the positioning and strategy fully take advantage of your opportunity?

5) How do you intend to position your product or service? How do your strategy and positioning work together?

6) How smart do your customers have to be to recognize the value of your sales proposition?

7) Are you currently in this business? Have you ever been involved with a similar business? How dynamic (broadly knowledgeable) and solid is your understanding of why some businesses in this category succeed, while others fail? What is the likelihood that previously successful market entry/business development strategies would work as well today?

8) How big is the actual market for your product or service -- how many of your prospective customers currently buy your product or service from someone? How quickly is the market projected to grow? How will your strategy support your short and longer term objectives?

9) What are the productivity and survival trends in this business category -- how much will it cost you to remain competitive?

10) What is the minimum market share you need to meet your financial objectives? How will you be able to reduce costs by achieving economies of scale as you move closer to achieving full production? How will your positioning and strategy function at different economic levels?

11) How are you making your strategy and positioning clear and understandable in words and action?

12) Who will be have full responsibility and accountability for implementing the strategy? What unique skills does the person have that will increase the likelihood of your business, product or service being a success?

13) How is your positioning and strategy unique and distinct compared to your competition? Have they been used together elsewhere in other situations, in different markets, or for different products or services? Can you speak with the person who was responsible for the effort, to learn what the results were -- and what the person would have done differently?

14) Are your positioning and strategy consistent with your business competencies and resources from a short-term and/or long-term perspective?

15) Are the major parts of your positioning and strategy consistent with other activities inside the organization? How can differences be managed and/or resolved? If your positioning and strategy represent a departure from past practices, will the new positioning or strategy create an level of risk that is acceptable and manageable in economic and personal terms?

16) Are your positioning and development strategy a good fit with the existing organizational culture?

17) What strategic concerns does developing this new product or service present for other parts of your organization? Will they be threatened by it? Will they be supportive? What reaction can you anticipate, and how do you intend to deal with it?

18) Is the strategy compatible with the personal values and goals of the key managers? Do you have strong, senior-level support?

19) How will the strategy and positioning inspire organizational effort and individual commitment?

20) Are there early indications of the responsiveness of the market and potential customers to your positioning and strategy? What kind of feedback are you getting?

21) How does the product or service positioning fit into your organization's overall market positioning and strategy?

22) Are you willing to invest sufficient energy and money to meet the competitive challenges that will threaten the successful development of this business? How far are you willing to go to support the positioning and strategy?

23) Who will make the final decision to support the positioning and strategy, and decide whether the organization should proceed or abandon the effort? What information will the person require to make the decision?

Suppliers – Sourcing

1) Are you willing to reduce the number of suppliers you deal with in exchange for more preferential treatment, i.e., better service or lower costs?

2) What alternatives are you exploring related to how you choose suppliers?

3) Do a small number of suppliers control your industry? If this is a significant problem, how can you circumvent or address the problem, i.e., long-term contracts, bring the function inside the organization, seek suppliers from outside of the region or country?

4) What are your built-in/fixed switching costs? Will your customers support your decision to switch your sources of supply?

5) What alternative products or services that you can use as a substitute are available?

6) Do your suppliers pose a significant threat of becoming your competitor? Have you considered requiring them to sign a non-compete agreement, or a non-disclosure agreement?

7) How important is your business to the supplier?

8) What is your supplier doing to add value to the working relationship?

9) What is your supplier doing to help you reduce costs, or gain a competitive advantage in the marketplace?

10) At what point are you involving your suppliers in new product or service development efforts?

11) How much does the supplier/service provider know about your business and business category?

12) What are the supplier's primary strengths – the reason you work with them?

13) How do you plan to start working with a new supplier? Will you:

- Give them all of your business?
- Give them a small assignment or project and see how well they do it?
- Give them a shadow assignment; give them the same assignment you give to your incumbent supplier and see how they would do it differently?
- Give them a big piece, i.e., an existing product line, brand, division, of your corporate business to work on?
- Give them your business in one of your markets, i.e., the USA, Latin America, European Union, Middle East, or ASEAN areas of the world?

14) Do you expect the supplier to develop new skills; do they know what you expect them to do?

15) How long will the supplier have to develop its new skill-set?

16) How much time, coaching, emotional and financial support are you willing to provide?

17) If you end the relationship, how much damage can the supplier cause your company if it goes to work for your competition?

18) How long have the people who currently work on your business at the supplier been assigned to your business? How long will they be assigned?

19) Do you personally like the people who the supplier has assigned to your business?

20) Will you miss the supplier's people if you have to end the relationship?

21) How willing is the supplier to commit time, money and effort to making the new business relationship work? What is the level of commitment across the supplier's organization? What percentage of the supplier's business does the amount of work you give them represent?

22) Based on past behavior, how willing is the supplier to work with your other suppliers? How have they demonstrated that willingness in their work with other clients?

23) How often does the supplier you're evaluating identify new opportunities to grow the business of its existing customers even if it doesn't immediately translate into new business or additional revenue for them?

24) If you end the relationship with your existing supplier, how confident are you of getting the same level of quality from the new supplier?

25) To what extent, do you owe the incumbent supplier your loyalty? How often have they gone above and beyond the call of duty to help you? If you're currently upset with them, do they know it? Are your problems with the supplier the result of one person's behavior, or are they part of a larger systemic problem the supplier is having?

26) What do other people inside your company think of the supplier's work who depend on it?

27) What are the *relevant* characteristics of the most successful working relationships you have entered into in the past?

28) How protective is the supplier of your confidential information? [Can you walk into empty meeting rooms and other easily accessible office spaces when visiting the prospective supplier, and look around to see what confidential, client/customer-sensitive information is left lying around that could easily be taken?]

29) Can the supplier keep a secret?

31) Are the supplier's best people assigned to your business? How responsive are they? How well do they anticipate your needs?

32) How has the supplier learned from its past mistakes?

33) Will the supplier's size limit your ability to grow? Is significant growth something you are anticipating as you move forward? Does having a big or small supplier matter to you?

34) If you shift part of your business, how do you intend to provide on-site technical support, supervision and staffing assistance to the new supplier who will assume the work from the incumbent supplier?

35) Do you intend to provide the supplier's staff with their own office/work space (including locks on the doors) on-site at your facilities on a dedicated basis?

36) Is there a general agreement regarding what both your organizations bring to the relation-ship, and what both of you expect to get out of it?

37) How flexible is the supplier in their staffing arrangements with you?

38) Can the supplier quickly draw upon a roster of outside experts and secondary suppliers or do they think they are great at everything?

39) What are the limits or restrictions on the use of the knowledge or intellectual property gained from the working relationship by either organization?

40) What factors do you regard as *controllable* in your current working relationship(s) with suppliers?

41) What factors do you regard as *uncontrollable*? Which factors will become more/less controllable if you switch suppliers?

42) How do you prospectively plan to initiate discussions with new suppliers, publicly or privately, directly or through a third party?

43) How long do you expect the supplier selection process to take? How many times do you expect to meet with prospective suppliers before you choose one?

44) Who at your organization will be responsible for making the new working relationship succeed, and how long will they be assigned to the project?

45) How far are you willing to travel when visiting the supplier? From a day-to-day operating perspective, can you utilize email and video-conferencing to avoid traveling?

46) When has the supplier acted on what they say is their strategic vision of the future? Are they consistent, or opportunistic?

47) When has the supplier staff failed to live up to what they said they were going to do?

48) Are there any obvious regional, national or multinational conflicts of interest with their other clients that would prevent or limit your opportunity to work together?

49) How consistent is the supplier's self-image? How is it perceived by other organizations with whom it does business?

50) What do former business partners have to say about the supplier? How has it settled disputes or disagreements with business partners in the past?

51) To what does the supplier attribute its history of growth? [If the supplier is a knowledge-based supplier, and they have grown through mergers or acquisitions, are the smart people still at the company, and productive? Where's the proof?]

52) What do knowledgeable outsiders consider to be the key factors, related to the supplier's growth, and how are they different from its own perceptions?

53) What not-readily-apparent potential liabilities does the supplier have?

54) How stable is the supplier? What is their annual staff turnover? How often do they lose clients/customers?

55) What are the backgrounds of the key managers, i.e., operations, finance, marketing, strategic planning, research and development, consulting, academia? How are they different from your own?

56) How are you taking organizational and cultural differences into consideration, regarding how you interpret information? [This can be especially important when dealing with suppliers in foreign countries.]

57) What explicit commitments is the supplier willing to make regarding the assignment of key personnel to your business?

58) Have you made your own reference checks, talking with at least three former supplier clients/customers, regarding why their relationship with the supplier ended?

59) Do you intend to use the same criteria you're using to evaluate prospective suppliers to make a side-by-side comparison with your current supplier(s)?

Worker and Operations Scheduling

1) Which of your customer's jobs/projects currently has top priority? How do you anticipate assignment of priorities will change in the next 30 days, 6 months or 18 months? Who assigns priorities, and how much control does the person have over the assignment of priorities? In practical terms, when a job/project is assigned 'priority' status, does everyone have a clear, consistent understanding of what that

means? Do people have a clear understanding of who the project leader is and who is directly responsible and accountable for getting various parts of a project completed? Do people understand how they (and others) will be held accountable?
2) What information do you need to more effectively manage operations and staff scheduling? How have you sought the cooperation of the operating staff [stakeholders] to look at the different staffing/scheduling options? What were the specific results?
3)   Is there an opportunity for people who work in teams to arrange their own schedules, i.e., work off-hours out of their homes, four 10-hour days, three 12-hour days, to front load production enabling people to get more time off during family holidays, hunting season, etc.?
4) Can people work shifts for other people or 'cover' for other employees who may be temporarily struggling with personal events in their lives? Are people directly involved with the effort being encouraged to identify what flexible options may exist?
5)   Are you providing and paying for office space for people, who with a little coaching, would be more productive and happier working at client locations, or out of their own homes?
6) If you have a staffing plan, how can you develop a more effective staff schedule?
7) In measurable terms, how large of an impact does your choice of priority assignment/dispatching/routing/allocating have on maintaining the overall operating effectiveness of your system? What percentage of your organization's total activities are managed on a variable or short term basis?
8) Are salaried employees permitted 'comp' time following completion of a particularly grueling project? What about other members of the organization?
Can you use a cafeteria-style incentive system to develop higher yield staffing arrangements, or to retain valued employees?

Work Evaluation

1) What standards of measurement can you use to compare alternative work flows or determine needs for future capacity? What percentage of daily activities on either an individual or collective basis are dedicated to value-added production (this includes focused research & development). What percentage of individual activities or collective activities are focused on *controllable* value-adding activities? What percentage of the activities as measured as a total percentage of time are *non-controllable* but clearly add value? How do other organizations measure work flow? What other friendly organizations can you talk with who have experience in this area?
2) What percentage of your measurable activities improve the prospect of the long term survival and growth of your organization, as distinguishable from effort

expended on increasing current billable hours or production focused on activities that do little to ensure the long term survivability or profitability of your organization?

[Current, or foreseeable short-term profitability is essential to any organization, but how is what you're measuring also taking into consideration the need for the organization to grow and evolve in a way that will ensure that a measurable percentage of the organization's activities are expended to develop the core drivers of future profitability and growth for the organization? Where are the large cash flows going to come from?]

3) Do your work measurement activities identify or recognize what non-controllable problems your employees have to deal with on a daily basis, i.e., those activities that just won't wait? Are work disruptions a predictable part of the business? As part of your measurement activities, are you measuring and evaluating people and business activities based on how people react in non-controllable or adverse situations involving down-time, or the ability to respond quickly or improvise and otherwise deal with uncertainty? How can you use your measurement activities to identify strategies for reducing the total number of hours involving non-controllable activities?
4) How are you estimating the amount of labor needed to develop a new product or service, and how do these estimates reconcile against traditional estimates, and current operating realities? How long do your estimates extend into the future – to the point of start-up, financial break-even? How do your estimates differ from that of your competition with regard to how quickly and inexpensively they can bring a product or service to market?
5) How will your project enjoy a competitive cost advantage or disadvantage related to allocation of overhead expenses, access to management expertise, production scheduling, sales support, or distribution? Can you shorten your time-to-market through the use of strategic alliances, joint operating agreements, patents, use of intellectual property rights, copyrights, franchisee/franchisor, or licensing agreements?
6) How much total production/sales volume do you need from your new product or service before your cost is low enough to be competitive in existing markets locally, regionally, or multinationally?
7) How will your methods of work measurement and evaluation change as you introduce more or less technology, or change your staffing mix? How do measurement and evaluation methods you're using influence what business development opportunities you evaluate?
8) Do your work measurement & evaluation metrics accurately channel employee activities where they currently are, or will be, most profitable and provide the greatest benefit to your organization?

Business Plan Outline:

1) Executive Summary
A) Assumptions About the Behavior of the Existing Market
B) A Description of the Business Idea and the Products or Services
C) The Size and Timeliness of the Opportunity
D) The Target Markets and Growth Projections
E) The Developmental Strategy
F) The Competitive Advantages
G) The Economics, Profitability, and Harvest Potential or Exit Strategy
H) The Management Team
I) The Public or Private Offering (Projected Date)

2) The Industry The Companies And Their Products Or Services
A) The Existing Industry/Business Sector Products and/or Service Category
B) Foreseeable Changes in the Existing Industry/Business Sector Products and/or Service Category
C) The Company and the Concept
D) The Product(s) or Service(s)
E) The Market Entry and Business Development/Growth Strategy

3) Market Research And Analysis
A) The Existing Customers for the Product(s) or Service(s)
B) The Estimated Market Size and Growth Trends
C) The Competition/Competitors – An Assessment of Competitive Advantages and Differences
D) Estimated/Projected Market Share and Sales Volume
E) Ongoing Market Tracking & Evaluation/Competitive Intelligence
F) Evaluation of Merger & Acquisition Candidates and/or Joint Venture Partners

4) The Economics Of The Business
A) The Gross and Net Operating Margins
B) The Profit Potential and Sustainability
C) The Fixed, Variable, and Semi-variable Costs – Timing of Cash Flows/Infusions
D) The Months to Breakeven
E) The Months to Reach Positive Cash Flow

5) Marketing Plan & Sales Plan
A) The Overall Marketing, Sales, Advertising & Corporate Communications Strategy
B) Pricing
C) Sales Staffing and Tactical Marketing Resource Allocation Scenarios
D) Customer Service and Warranty Policies

    E) Advertising, Promotion, Public Relations

    F) Distribution Channels, Joint Ventures & Joint Operating Agreements – Selection of Channel Marketing Partners

    G) E-commerce

6) Design And Development Plans

    A) On-Going Development, Critical Tasks/Hurdles and Progress Tracking

    B) Assessment of Difficulties and Risks

    C) Product/Service Improvement Options

    D) Fixed, Semi-Variable and Variable Costs

    E) Proprietary Issues

7) Manufacturing And Operations Plan

    A) The Annual Operating Plan

    B) The Geographic Location(s)

    C) The Facilities and Necessary Improvements

    D) Manufacturing Strategy and Planning

    E) The Regulatory and Legal Issues

8) Management Team

    A) The Organization Structure

    B) The Key Management People

    C) Management Compensation and Ownership

    D) The Active and Passive Investors

    E) Employment Contracts, Stock Options, Bonus Plans, and Other Incentives

    F) The Board of Directors/Trustees

    G) Shareholder Rights and Restrictions

    H) Professional Advisors and Outside Service Providers

9) Overall/Master Development Schedule

10) Major Critical Risk Factors, Potential Operating Problems, And Marketplace Assumptions

11) The Financial Plan

    A) On-Going Income Statements and Balance Sheets

    B) Pro Forma Income Statements

    C) Pro Forma Balance Sheets

    D) Pro Forma Cash Flow Analysis

    E) Breakeven Charts and Calculations

    F) Cost Controls

G) Summary Estimates and Calculations

H) Assumptions, Benchmark Validations/Justifications

12) Proposed Company Offering

A) Financing Being Sought – an Evaluation of Alternative Financing Options/Strategies

B) Offering

C) Capitalization

D) Use of Funds

E) Investors' Return on Investment

13) Appendices

*   *   *

Author and Publisher: Kerry James O'Connor
6800 North Clunbury Road
West Bloomfield, MI 48322-4315 USA

Em: kerryjamesoconnor@gmail.com   ISBN: 978-0-6151-6863-0

© Kerry O'Connor 1992, 1997, 1998, 2000, 2001, 2003, 2007   All rights reserved. This book, or parts thereof, may not be reproduced in any form without permission from the publisher.

www.ingramcontent.com/pod-product-compliance
Lightning Source LLC
Chambersburg PA
CBHW051352200326
41521CB00014B/2549